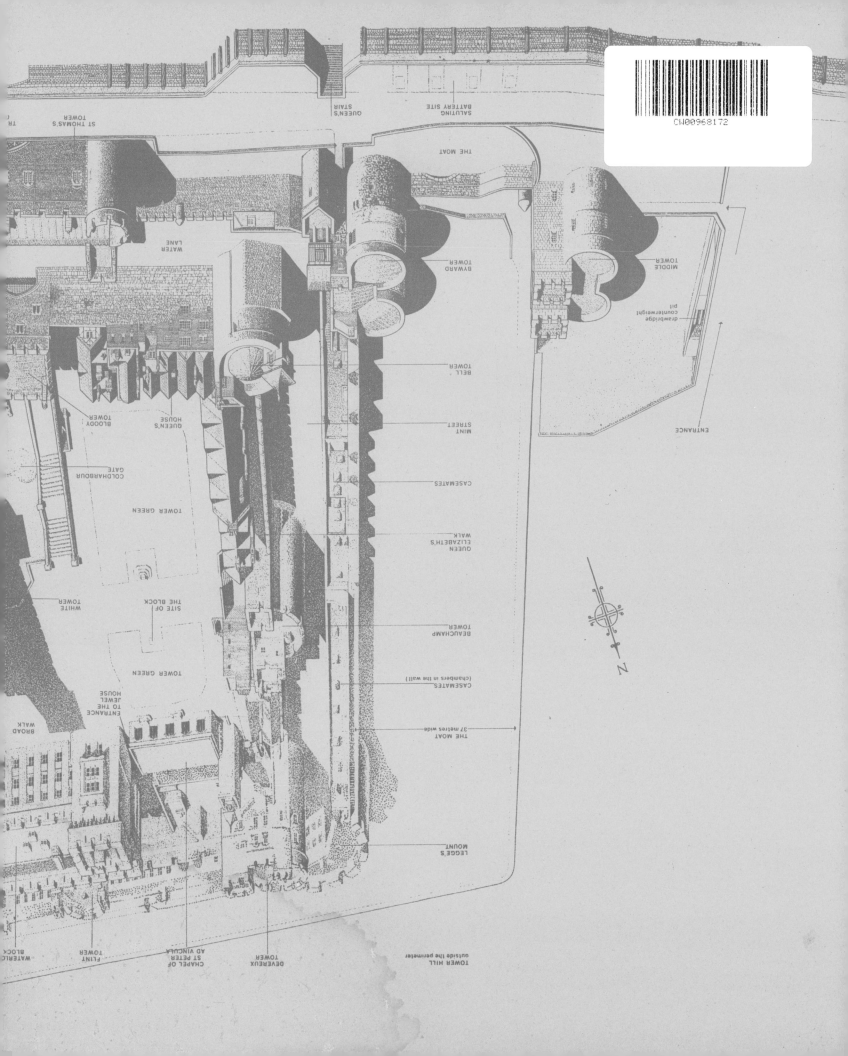

ST THOMAS'S TOWER

QUEEN'S STAIR

SALUTING BATTERY SITE

THE MOAT

WATER LANE

BYWARD TOWER

MIDDLE TOWER

drawbridge counterweight pit

BELL TOWER

BLOODY TOWER

MINT STREET

COLDHARBOUR GATE

QUEEN'S HOUSE

ENTRANCE

CASEMATES

TOWER GREEN

QUEEN ELIZABETH'S WALK

WHITE TOWER

SITE OF THE BLOCK

TOWER GREEN

BEAUCHAMP TOWER

ENTRANCE TO THE JEWEL HOUSE

CASEMATES (chambers in the wall)

BROAD WALK

THE MOAT 37 metres wide

N

LEGGE'S MOUNT

WATERLOO BLOCK

FLINT TOWER

CHAPEL OF ST PETER AD VINCULA

DEVEREUX TOWER

TOWER HILL outside the perimeter

# THE
# TOWER
## OF
# LONDON

900 YEARS OF ENGLISH HISTORY

KENNETH J. MEARS

*Photographs by*
*Lark Gilmer*

PHAIDON · OXFORD

*Photographic Acknowledgements*

With the exception of those listed below, the
photographs in the book are by Lark Gilmer.
The illustrations on pp. 139 and 143 are by courtesy of
the Royal Armouries; those on pp. 97, 101, 144, 147,
148, 149, 151 and 155 are Crown Copyright.

Phaidon Press Limited
Littlegate House
St Ebbe's Street
Oxford
OX1 1SQ

First published 1988

© 1988 by Phaidon Press Limited

British Library Cataloguing in Publication Data

Mears, Kenneth J.
    The Tower of London : 900 years of
    English history.
    1. Tower of London — history
    I. Title
    942.1′5            DA687.T7

ISBN 0-7148-2527-1

Printed and bound in England by Butler and Tanner
Limited, Frome

*Frontispiece illustrations*

*Page 1: A corridor in St Thomas's Tower.*

*Title-page: The east side of the White Tower at dusk.*

*Pages 6-7: The day beginning on Tower Wharf, with Tower Bridge in the
background.*

# Contents

# *Preface*

My wife and I joined the Tower in December of 1979 and moved into St Thomas's Tower (the oldest duplex apartment in the United Kingdom, *circa* 1280). Unfortunately, it required a major refurbishment to protect us from the elements and, as there was no other accommodation, we had to move from room to room while the Property Services Agency did their best and worst. In all, it took fifteen months to complete the work and gave us firsthand experience of living on a building site. Perhaps, the most hilarious moment was when a tourist rang the front door bell and said, 'Do you know that you are filling the moat with silicon chips?' Some of the 250 sacks of roof insulation had found its way through the old cracked beams and was creating an artificial hailstorm to the amazement of passing visitors.

Our morale was boosted by the resident ghost who used to frighten the occasional workman by opening the front door and walking through the house to the Oratory (dedicated to Thomas Becket and off our main bedroom). We think he was trying to help my wife clean up after the daily mess made by painters, plumbers and electricians, although he was not see by them, but often heard. Subsequently, he appeared to a friend of my wife, dressed in a brown cassock and carrying a bucket; other viewings have been quite precise over the past century and a half, the last being when seen by three witnesses including the present Chief Yeoman Warder.

My wife, Elizabeth, inspired this book and has been responsible for the secretarial work and

*St Thomas's Tower by night.*

much of the proof reading. As always, I am in her debt. Peter Hammond, the Education Officer of the Tower, gave invaluable help in checking the historical accuracy of the text and, as a fellow author, recognized the problems posed in compressing such a wide swathe of English history. Lark Gilmer has made the text come alive, her photography is a joy, and may I thank the Tower authorities, the Royal Armouries, the Military Guard, the Brass Mount, the Yeoman Body and all who co-operated with her when she strived for perfection. The Lord Chamberlain's Office, in particular Marcus Bishop, have been encouraging and helpful as, indeed, have my colleagues in the Department of the Environment. Finally, I must make mention of Peter Clayton, a renowned Egyptologist and friend, who convinced me that 900 years of history was a drop in the ocean compared with his speciality; he had faith in my synopsis, which, in his terms, was modern history.

*The Tower of London* has evolved from my experience of living and working there over the past decade, and covers the history of the Tower, the Crown Jewels and the Royal Armouries. It is a personal view which includes the anecdotes, the ghosts, the legends and, above all, the atmosphere which comes from being a member of the Tower community. Think of it as the story of a castle, the houses within the castle, and the people who have lived and died there. Not.'900 years of blood and torture' but '900 years of village history' – a village which parallels the history of England itself.

# I
# *Building a Castle*
## 1066–1307

William the Conqueror was a bastard. No, this is not an outburst from a disgruntled contemporary, but a fact which coloured much of his early life and helped to form the rugged character that was to have such an effect on early English history. William's father was Robert Count of Hiesmois, later first Duke of Normandy; his mother was Arlette, the daughter of a tanner in Falaise. William was probably born between October and December 1027, certainly not later than 1028. The story of his parentage was well known and William was taunted by cries of 'Hides for the tanner!' by the citizens of Alençon in the siege of 1049. Such were the inauspicious beginnings of William the Conqueror, the builder of the Tower of London and the architect of the Norman conquest of England.

How did it all happen? The contrasting claims of Harold and William to the throne of England on the death of the childless Edward the Confessor in January 1066 form a separate story. In essence, William believed that Harold would support his claim to the throne as Edward's designated heir—Harold is alleged to have sworn an oath to this effect—but Edward revoked his earlier promise on his deathbed and named Harold as his successor. The scene was set for conflict, culminating in the battle of Hastings on 15 October 1066. As an ex-cavalryman I can admire William's tactics which exploited the weakness of unsupported infantry against heavy cavalry and archers. The battle over, and

*Morning sun on Beauchamp Tower*

Harold's body laid on the shores of Sussex, William moved rapidly — first to Romney, where he extracted vengeance for the killing of some of his troops who had been isolated there, thence to Dover.

Dover marked the consolidation of his landing and, despite his efforts to avoid looting, William had some problem in controlling his troops. To them Dover was a fat cow for the milking. Canterbury surrendered and there was then a temporary halt as William fell ill for about a month. During this illness he was given the good news that Winchester, the capital of Wessex, had submitted. This city formed part of the dowry of Edward the Confessor's wife, Eadgyth, and William was well content to leave her in control. By December he was en route for London but, apart from burning Southwark to the ground after a foray by some knights from the city, William made no attempt to cross the river as he judged it too costly an operation. Instead, he made a wide sweep to the west and crossed at Wallingford. Stigand, the Archbishop of Canterbury, decided that discretion was the better part of valour and submitted; London followed suit. On Christmas Day William was crowned by Archbishop Ealdred of York in Westminster Abbey, amid scenes of some unrest.

London was the largest of the walled cities in a feudal society where the majority of the inhabitants lived on the land. These cities were tiny, compared to those of today, and London

numbered some 20,000 inhabitants from a total population of, perhaps, a million and a half. The greater part of the city consisted of wooden houses, roofed with straw. Fire was always a serious threat and soon stone and tiles were used instead. William decided to build forts to dominate London and the river, which was a major trade artery. One was established at the south-eastern corner of the city where the old Roman city wall (circa AD 200) joined the later Roman river wall (circa AD 395) which ran west to Blackfriars making a 'vee'. These walls were almost 20 feet (6 m) high and formed formidable obstacles in themselves. The addition of a Norman fort with its palisades, earthworks and ditch would give William a safe haven, and until it was completed he stayed outside London at Barking.

It was only a matter of time before William needed a palace as well as a fortress and by 1078 he had decided to replace the wooden fort by a truly substantial building; he authorised the construction of what is now known as the White Tower which took some twenty years to complete, the architect being a Norman abbot, Gundulf of Bec, Bishop of Rochester. This may seem strange but stone buildings of this period were predominantly ecclesiastical and the expertise in building lay with the clergy.

The building itself is massive being some 118 feet (36 m) east to west, 107 feet (32.5 m) north to south, and 90 feet (27.5 m) high to the battlements, with the turrets being additional. The turrets are square, with the exception of the north-east, which is cylindrical containing the main spiral staircase to the base. The bulk of the building material is Kentish ragstone but limestone from Caen was imported to strengthen vital areas, particularly at the corners. The limestone was planed smooth and was clearly distinguishable from the rougher Kentish rag. Later, in 1240, the whole Tower was whitewashed (hence, 'the White Tower') and it became a magnificent and dominating sight. It was one of the first stone keeps to be raised by the Normans in England and had only one entrance, high on the south side, reached by a wooden

*The White Tower, c. 1078. The wooden staircase is in the same position as the original, which was removable for additional security.*

staircase. This staircase could be removed when trouble threatened and, as an added precaution, the circular staircase leading from the basement to the north-east turret mounts in a clockwise direction so that any defender had free use of his right sword arm. The present external wooden staircase to the first floor is similarly positioned to the original. The White Tower had windows rather than arrow slits; originally narrow, these windows were widened, principally in the eighteenth century, leaving only two pairs to remind us of Gundulf's work—immediately above the south entrance. Up to that time, the English castles had been of the 'motte and bailey' type (mound and enclosure) constructed of wood and surrounded by a ditch. These were gradually replaced by stone castles, the White Tower being a fore-runner.

Internally, the building consisted of a basement and two floors. The basement contains a well and was primarily used for storage. The two floors were separate residential apartments of considerable size with the upper being far the more palatial and including the Chapel of St John, a truly magnificent, plain austere Romanesque chapel lined with fine limestone from Caen, with twelve massive round columns, some of which are decorated with a T-shaped cross. This penthouse area and chapel was the King's residence; it included a gallery, part of which is still visible in the Chapel of St John today. Sometime, possibly as late as 1600, a third floor was added, at the level of this gallery, giving the three floors that are found in the White Tower today. The original floors were divided into three, including a hall, and were further sub-divided to taste. Nothing remains of the original decorations but emphasis was placed on the 'palace' rather than the 'fortress' of the Tower of London. The King's rooms with their high ceilings must have been most impressive and, combined with the Chapel of St John, Norman splendour was at its best. (The Chapel was misused as a storehouse during the eighteenth century, but was restored to its former style in Victorian times and still retains royal links. Prince Charles received Communion there on

his twenty-first birthday with his grandmother, Queen Elizabeth the Queen Mother, and his sister Princess Anne, now the Princess Royal.)

The first, or entrance, floor was allocated to the Constable who was, in effect, the Chief Executive of the Tower. Servants slept and ate in the halls of both apartments and in the basement; there were also outhouses alongside the White Tower to cater for additional soldiers and staff. As always the Tower was short of space.

Important though the White Tower was, it was only one of many residences owned or used by the king. Medieval kings travelled constantly with large retinues, partly to keep their subjects in order, sometimes for pleasure and hunting, and, occasionally, to wage war in border areas and overseas. The importance of the White Tower was related to its location in the most powerful of the walled cities and to its impregnability, when the monarch needed a safe haven.

The first Constable of the Tower was Geoffrey de Mandeville who was the nominee of William the Conqueror. He has been followed by 155 successors to date (1988) although there were none in the reign of Elizabeth I (who was not fond of the Tower) and there were gaps in the seventeenth century. Nowadays the Constable is normally a retired Field Marshal but it was not until 1784 that it became firm policy for the post to be held by a senior Army officer. Before that it had been held by many great Lords, both spiritual and temporal, including three Archbishops of Canterbury—Thomas Becket, Hubert Walter and Stephen Langton. In a less spiritual sphere, John Holland, the Duke of Exeter, a soldier at Agincourt, was a notorious Constable. Many prisoners were introduced to the 'Duke of Exeter's daughter', a nickname for the rack, the instrument of torture that stretched prisoners until their arms and legs left their sockets.

The powers of the Constable make interesting reading in this day and age. He has direct access to the Sovereign (rarely exercised but a significant right). Until Wellington abolished the custom, he could sell the appointment of Yeoman Warder if a Yeoman Warder died in

*The Tower of London, c.1100. William I positioned his fortress and palace about half a mile east (downstream) of the wooden bridge over the Thames and in the angle of the old Roman city and river walls, completing his defences with a dry ditch and palisade, soon to be replaced with a stone curtain wall. The ground-plan shows the division of the White Tower into three sections. The circular turret at the northeast corner contains the internal spiral staircase; the protruding semi-circular corner at the southeast accommodates the Chapel of St John on the second floor, with a crypt and sub-crypt below it.*

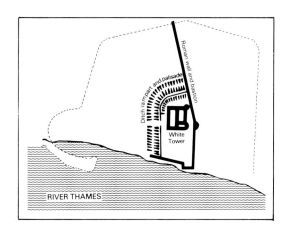

RIVER THAMES

*The austere Chapel of St John inside the White Tower. The walls are lined with the finest limestone from Caen.*

Tower service. From this comes the toast proposed to every new Yeoman Warder: 'May you never die a Yeoman Warder!' It was a great loss to the Warder's family, and an equivalent gain to the Constable, if a Yeoman Warder wrongly guessed his state of health and did not sell his appointment himself before he died. State prisoners paid fees to the Constable and he extracted a toll on such items as wine, oysters, mussels and cockles. He owned any cattle that fell off London Bridge, or swans that swam in the reaches below it. He also levied a fine of 6s. 8d. on ships that discharged their guns in the Thames and disturbed the Tower inhabitants. Would that the same could be done to the helicopters which plague us today! Twice over recent years the Royal Navy have re-enacted the ceremony of presenting a barrel of port to the Constable.

Initially the Constable lived in the White Tower, but it is unclear where he lived in later periods. There was a Constable's Tower (but there is some doubt whether he used it), the Constable's House by the Lanthorn Tower (but this was used by the Major of the Tower, a more junior officer) and the dwelling now known as Queen's House.

The first knowledge we have of a deputy is as early as 1198 when there is mention of the Lieutenant. There is only sketchy knowledge until the time of Henry VIII, but in the early seventeenth century the Constable's local powers were devolved to the Lieutenant, who became the Governor of the Tower (the term Resident Governor was not used until 1858). He lived in Queen's House, then known as the Lieutenant's Lodgings. The Constable retained his policy powers as he does to this day. After the time of William and Mary (1688–1702), the post of Lieutenant gradually became a sinecure and the duties were delegated to a Deputy Lieutenant, who dealt with State prisoners, and a Major, who handled other administration. By 1858 the post of 'Major and Resident Governor of the Tower' had evolved, now held by a retired Major General. The Lieutenant (now a retired Lieutenant General) takes part in the parade for the accession of a Constable (every five years), but otherwise only deputises when the Constable is absent. Neither the Constable nor the Lieutenant live in the Tower and they are not paid for their duties. The Resident Governor is the Chief Executive Officer of the Tower and is also the Keeper of the Jewel House as this post was amalgamated with his in 1967. He is supported by two Deputy Governors, one of whom is a serving officer of the Royal Army Ordnance Corps, as there is still an Ordnance store within the Tower. The doctor and the chaplain are both part-time and live alongside each other, providing a comprehensive service for Tower residents!

The Tower was not designed as a prison, but like many castles it was soon used as one. An early prisoner of note was the chief minister to William Rufus and the Tower's second chief architect and administrator, Ranulf Flambard, bishop of Durham, who reached his post by flattery and deceit. He was a dishonest, arrogant man who was finally brought to book for selling Church appointments to the highest bidder. After the death of William Rufus in 1100, Henry I could hardly wait to put Flambard in the Tower. Flambard was very fond of his food and the 2s. a day prison maintenance to cover accommodation, servants and food was enhanced considerably from his private means. He dined and wined well in the upper floors of the White Tower and when he decided to escape, had a rope smuggled into his quarters in a cask of

*The 'Major and Resident Governor of the Tower' in conversation with the Chaplain after the Christmas State Parade.*

wine. He wined his gaolers well and despite his bulk—he was a very heavy man—he squeezed through a window, lowered himself to the ground, clambered over the earthworks, and was met by friends who put him on board ship for Normandy. (Some years later he was pardoned and returned to England where he worked on the building of Durham Cathedral.)

The twelfth century saw little building work in the Tower, other than repairs. There were many royal castles and monarchs moved around the country with their entourage, rarely staying for long in one location. After Flambard had been disgraced the Tower was put in the hands of William de Mandeville, the son of the first Constable; he put right the storm and earthquake damage that had occurred over the past twenty years. He was succeeded in turn by his own son Geoffrey.

The very beginning of the century saw the building of the first Chapel of St Peter ad Vincula. The King had his own chapel, the Chapel of St John, in the White Tower and would often have an oratory, close to his sleeping quarters, for his private devotions. His entourage would not be allowed to use these and needed a parish church. This was of some size and was located just outside the ramparts (it was about a chapel's width to the north of the present Chapel Royal which dates from the sixteenth century). About 1110, on 1 August, it was consecrated and named 'St Peter ad Vincula' (St Peter in Chains) to commemorate the showing of St Peter's chains every year by the famous Roman Church of San Pietro in Vincoli. The present Chapel of St Peter ad Vincula was built in the time of Henry VIII, between the years 1513 and 1519, and became a Chapel Royal as late as 1967. (The Chapel of St John is not used for regular services, apart from the celebration of Holy Communion at Christmas, Easter and Whitsun.)

Stephen, the grandson of William the Conqueror, and son of the sister of Henry I, was chosen by the barons to succeed Henry who died in 1135—this was hotly disputed by Henry's daughter Matilda. Civil war dragged on until

1142 and the Tower came under siege for the first time when the City of London tried to dislodge the Constable, Geoffrey de Mandeville, Earl of Essex, who was a supporter of Matilda. The Tower was much too strong to fall, but might be starved into submission, so Geoffrey decided to escape, in company with a body of armed men, who proceeded to lay waste the country to the north of London. Stephen caught up with him at St Albans but, despite being tried for treason, Geoffrey managed to secure his freedom once again. The saga ended when he was killed by an arrow in a skirmish around Mildenhall. Stephen himself died in 1154 shortly after accepting Matilda's son, Henry, as his heir. Before Stephen's reign the Tower was just one of several royal southern castles such as Dover, Winchester and Windsor but its importance increased as it became the most secure base of them all.

Henry II was a man of ceaseless energy and knew all about building castles. He overhauled all the royal fortresses with a veritable army of masons and carpenters. Thomas Becket was charged with the task, but he was murdered at Canterbury Cathedral in 1170 before much was done to the Tower. Repairs were completed after his death. During this phase, Henry extended Westminster Abbey and, in the course of doing so had Edward the Confessor re-interred there, in a more impressive site. On the 13 October 1163, he was present when Bishop Lawrence took the sapphire ring from the finger of Edward the Confessor—the sapphire is now in the Maltese cross on top of the Imperial State Crown worn by the Queen at the State Opening of Parliament.

Records of work done at the Tower during the twelfth century are scanty and much of what is known is informed guesswork, though there are some interesting pointers, particularly relating to the King's residence. The White Tower was the refuge if attacked but its defensive design made it none too comfortable as a palace, and kings like their comfort. 'Houses within the castle' were certain to be demanded as the castle boundaries became stronger. Bills exist which describe repairs to the 'King's houses within the bailey',

*A window in the Beauchamp Tower.*

Henry II starting the trend, to be followed so successfully by his grandson, Henry III, of making the Sovereign both comfortable and safe.

It seems likely that the Wardrobe Tower was built at this time although building may have overlapped into the reigns of Richard I and John. The size of a king's entourage made it useful to establish stores of essential clothing, arms, equipment and even jewels at safe havens throughout the country. The Wardrobe Tower was such a depot and contained the King's treasury, as well as clothing, armour and equipment. The King's jewels were an important part of his power and were used as guarantees for loans as well as for displays of pomp and pageantry. The Regalia, used specifically for a coronation, was kept at Westminster Abbey but every king had, as Queen Elizabeth II has today, a considerable quantity of personal jewellery, gold and silver plate, and, of course, what might be termed his everyday crowns, since medieval kings wore a crown on most public or business appearances. The ruins of the Wardrobe Tower can still be seen to the east of the White Tower.

Henry II was succeeded by his son Richard I (1189–99), the 'Lionheart', who was in England for only five months of his reign, the period being dominated by his younger brother John. John was devious, unscrupulous, untrustworthy and ruthless—not an attractive character, and Richard's chancellor William Longchamp was hardly better. He was arrogant and unpopular but had risen to the positions of Bishop of Ely, Justiciar of all England, and Constable of the Tower. He spoke no English but was intensely loyal to Richard and realised the danger of John's ambitions while the King was absent at the Crusades. He decided, for his own safety, to make the Tower impregnable.

Longchamp's plans were ambitious but not altogether successful. He started the building of the tower now known as the Bell Tower, and built eastwards extending the river wall to form a curtain wall, as far as the present Bloody Tower. He also extended the curtain wall northwards as far as the present Beauchamp Tower, and then east to join the old city wall alongside the White

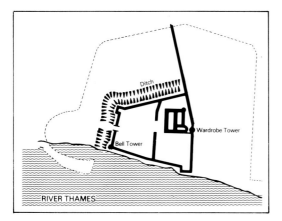

Ditch
Wardrobe Tower
Bell Tower
RIVER THAMES

The Tower of London, c. 1200. The Tower has been extended westwards, the earlier ditch has been filled in, new external walls have been built and the northern and western sides are defended by Bishop Longchamp's ambitious but unsuccessful ditch. With the exception of the Bell Tower and the ruins of the Wardrobe Tower, built on the foundations of an earlier Roman bastion, nothing remains above ground of the new building work of the twelfth century. The king's houses were immediately to the south of the White Tower. The parish church of St Peter ad Vincula was just outside the ditch at the northwest corner.

Tower, which Longchamp may have rebuilt. He also dug a ditch which was intended to be a moat but his knowledge of sluices did not match his other building expertise, and the ditch filled and emptied with the ebb and flow of the Thames. It is also possible that Longchamp completed, or at least refurbished, the Wardrobe Tower started by Henry II.

The feud between King John and Longchamp came to a head in 1191. John laid siege to the Tower; Longchamp lost his nerve and surrendered. Building work within the Tower came to a halt but in 1199 John resumed the construction of the Bell Tower which was completed in about 1200. Longchamp escaped to the Continent and remained in exile.

The Bell Tower is some 60 feet (18 m) high and has an 18 foot (5½ m) solid plinth. It is unusual for the time, being of a circular rather than a rectangular design, and the arrow slits are cleverly designed to deflect an attacker's shafts. In recent years an expert bowman tried to shoot an arrow in through one of these slits but had to confess himself beaten. The alarm bell was fitted in 1532 but the present bell is of a later date and, with its housing, was installed in 1651. The Tudor 'Lieutenant's Lodgings' (today called Queen's House) was built on to the Bell Tower and the previous internal staircase was removed so that access to the two chambers (known as the Upper and Lower Bell) could be obtained only through the Resident Governor's house. These rooms were reserved for very important prisoners

The Bell Tower, c. 1200. The present bell turret dates from the seventeenth century.

(Overleaf) Part of Henry III's wall linking the Wakefield Tower and the Coldharbour Gate (no longer standing). In the background is the wall walk linking the Lanthorn Tower and Wakefield Tower.

such as Princess Elizabeth, Thomas More, John Fisher, Arabella (Arbella) Stuart, and the Duke of Monmouth.

King John was crowned in 1199 by the Archbishop of Canterbury, Hubert Walter. The Anointing Spoon used at John's coronation is displayed at the Jewel House today and has the distinction of being the oldest surviving piece of the Regalia, most of which had to be replaced by Charles II because Parliament had sold, or melted down, the King's treasury after the execution of Charles I. When Hubert Walter's tomb was opened, a small chalice, now on display in Canterbury Cathedral, was found, the designs on which exactly match the designs on the bowl of the spoon. The spoon survived as it was kept by a Mr Clement Kynnersley, who bought it for the sum of 16s on 27 December 1649. (He was a Yeoman of the Removing Wardrobe to Charles I and was reinstated into the same appointment on the restoration of Charles II. He must have sold the spoon back to the Crown Jeweller, Sir Thomas Viner, and made a profit on the deal as it was priced then at £2.)

John's reign continued as it had begun—stormy. In 1215, having been forced by the barons into granting Magna Carta at Runnymede, John had to surrender control of the Tower, as a pledge of good behaviour. However, he had not the least intention of keeping to the terms of this agreement and civil war was inevitable. The barons invited the Dauphin, Prince Louis, the French King's heir, to take the throne, on the tenuous grounds of his marriage to a granddaughter of Henry II, and he took up residence at the Tower while the King retreated to Winchester. John was also the first monarch to lose the Crown Jewels. While fighting a series of skirmishes in East Anglia, in October 1216, his baggage train fell victim to quicksands as he was en route to Lincolnshire. A few days later John died, worn out by debauchery, overeating and drinking, at the age of forty-eight. His nine-year-old son Henry was crowned at Gloucester with a makeshift gold circlet, the civil war ended, and Louis withdrew to France.

Henry III (1216–72) was a man who loved

beauty and elegance—not for him the blood-thirsty campaigning of his predecessors. During his minority he was guided by three Regents, of whom Hubert de Burgh was the most prominent, acting much in the guise of a favourite uncle. Castles and fortresses had become vulnerable to the new siege weapons available and to the sophisticated siege craft employed. Once again the time had come to strengthen defences and review existing fortifications. The general plan for the Tower of London was to surround the White Tower with a ring of further towers and curtain walls, expand the area where necessary, and encircle the whole with a moat fed from the Thames and properly controlled. By the time Henry was thirteen the work was started and he began to take a keen personal interest, eventually taking over control of the whole project himself. He spared no money and the Tower was inundated with craftsmen and labourers throughout his reign. Henry was a deeply religious man and his building activities were not confined to the Tower. It was he who gave us Salisbury Cathedral and, because he felt a deep religious affinity for Edward the Confessor, rebuilt Westminster Abbey, a masterpiece of Gothic architecture with its raised platform for coronations of the kings of England, and re-interred him there for the second time. He also built Westminster Palace, which became the main administrative capital, and the Tower, being fortified, was used for other departments and as a defensive haven.

The Regents started the work by rebuilding and refurbishing the palace buildings south of the White Tower. There is mention of the Great Hall and the King's Chamber, which were in the area now occupied by the History Gallery. The Wakefield Tower was started, which was to contain an oratory, and become the King's Privy Chamber with direct access to the Great Hall. This Tower also formed the main defence for the water entrance to the Tower and, to complete the watergate, what became the lower half of the Bloody Tower was built, the upper half not being completed until the reign of Edward I. There was also a small, private watergate to the east of the Wakefield Tower which was used by the King.

*The Bloody Tower. Once known as the Garden Tower, because of its proximity to the Lieutenant's gardens, it earned its worldwide notoriety from Shakespeare's King Richard III and the mystery surrounding the fate of the two young princes.*

Nothing remains of the Great Hall and its style is pure conjecture. It would have been the focal point of palace life and is likely to have been a wooden-roofed building with glazed windows and a central fireplace. It was rebuilt in 1230 and both it and the White Tower were whitewashed, the latter in 1240. It was this whitewashing that gave the White Tower its name and it must have been an awe-inspiring sight. No wonder the City of London was nervous! There is mention of the Queen's Chamber being whitewashed and painted with flowers—this probably formed part of the buildings running south from the Wardrobe Tower to the Great Hall. The Wardrobe Tower, where the King kept his costly possessions, was also refurbished around this period. In 1244 it also held the Crown Jewels and Regalia as a temporary measure while Westminster Abbey was being rebuilt. The palace was also guarded by another gate, the Coldharbour Gate (which no longer exists) north of the Wakefield Tower, so the Inner Ward was a defensive entity within the overall Tower defences.

To enlarge and strengthen the Tower as a stronghold in his disputes with the barons Henry built eleven towers, although one fell down and had to be rebuilt by his son, Edward I. Each had its own design and purpose and, to save confusion, present-day names are used in the descriptions that follow. The White Tower itself, apart from being whitewashed, was given a wooden gallery so that archers could shoot directly down at any enemy who might reach the base of the Tower. It was the last bastion of defence and was immensely strong.

The Wakefield Tower, like most of the towers, had residential accommodation on the top floor—the lower floor where arrow slits predominate, being reserved for the men-at-arms. Originally, it was called the Blundeville Tower and was built in two phases between 1220 and 1240, standing at the river's edge, the Thames being wider than today. This Tower was linked to the Lanthorn Tower by a curtain wall, the Lanthorn being at the junction of the Roman city wall and the river wall. Its name evolved

from its use as a signalling post to ships and as a navigational aid at night. Later it came to contain or adjoin the royal apartments. It was damaged by fire in 1774, demolished in 1777, and replaced by a nineteenth-century tower of the same name.

Hitherto all the work had been within the area of existing Tower land but by 1240 further expansion was needed. The Roman wall was breached, and land was bought from the Master of St Katharine's Hospital to the east and from the Prior of Holy Trinity Aldgate to the west, and the next great phase was started. Longchamp's wall to the north of the Bell Tower was re-constituted and a new land entrance built (where the Beauchamp Tower is today). On the night of 23 April 1240, this landgate fell down, and on the same day a year later the wall to the south of it also collapsed. It was said that the ghost of Thomas Becket was seen on both occasions, beating the stones with his crozier, taking revenge for his murder in Canterbury (he had been Constable of the Tower and considered it part of his personal domain). 'You will never build here', he said.

Going eastwards from the Lanthorn Tower, the Salt Tower was built. At one time it was used for salt storage, indeed salt still lingers in the walls, but, originally, it was intended for defence and accommodation. All the towers have been used for prisoners although none were built specifically for this purpose. The inscriptions on the walls within give an idea of those most frequently used. The Tower was never a common prison in the mode of the Marshalsea, the Fleet, or the Clink, and prisoners had to be distinguished, either because of their high rank, or their offence—treason—or, very often, both, in order to be lodged there. Ghosts are a way of life with the Salt Tower and there are some Yeoman Warders who will not approach it late at night. There are many inscriptions, several by luckless Jesuits who were tortured and executed. These unfortunates are said to haunt the precincts casting stones at sentries, and have occasionally been seen in their ancient dress. Although used as a prison in Tudor times, the Salt Tower's

*The Wakefield Tower. This tower was used as a royal residence for much of the later Middle Ages and was part of the medieval palace. It was here that Henry VI was murdered.*

accommodation origin is shown by the thirteenth-century fireplace which still exists on the first floor.

The rooms of the next tower, the Broad Arrow, also contain inscriptions denoting that they were used as prison cells; the following tower, the Constable, appears to have remained as accommodation only. The Constable Tower was rebuilt in the nineteenth century and the upper part of the Broad Arrow Tower has had considerable restoration work.

The Martin Tower, being at the angle of the walls, is much more dominating than the others and projects to give better fields of fire. Here again inscriptions show where prisoners have been held, but this tower became better known as the home of the Crown Jewels from 1669 to the early nineteenth century, and it was from here that Colonel Blood made his attempt to steal them in 1671.

The Brick and Bowyer Towers are both, to a greater or lesser extent, nineteenth-century reconstructions of Henry's work and, together with the Flint and Devereux Towers, they were originally for accommodation although later used for prisoners by the Tudors. The Devereux, like the Martin, is an angle tower; it both dominates and projects to give excellent fields of fire. Outside the new curtain wall a new Moat was dug by John le Fosseur who understood sluices; the tidal effects of the Thames were controlled, keeping the Moat full at all times, and also enabling it to be flushed twice daily—very necessary, as it was the repository for all the sewage.

Much else was happening while all this building was progressing. Poor Hubert de Burgh, the Justiciar, found that Henry III had inherited some of John's bad qualities when he was deprived of his titles and lands in 1232. He fled to Brentwood in Essex and claimed sanctuary. Henry had him starved out and thrown into the Tower in chains. Fortunately, Henry's bad temper did not last long, but de Burgh never regained his place of power although he was restored to royal favour after two years.

The first recorded use of the Tower as a

*The Salt Tower. During the
Tudor period this was a prison of
ill repute, frequently used for the
incarceration of Roman Catholic
priests.*

menagerie was in 1235 when Henry placed three leopards there, a present from Emperor Frederick II. In 1251 the King of Norway sent a polar bear (with its keeper) and it used to be seen fishing for salmon in the Thames, complete with collar and long lead. Henry ordered the Sheriffs of London to pay 4d a day for its upkeep. This was not the first royal menagerie as Henry I had established a wildlife park at Woodstock in 1100, and animals from there were transferred to the Tower to augment the growing collection. In 1255, an elephant arrived as a present from Louis IX of France; an elephant house was built, some 40 × 20 feet (12 m × 6 m), and the public flocked to see this strange beast. Unfortunately the elephant did not take to the English climate, or to English food, and died after two years. We do not know the location of the Menagerie at this time, although it must have been within the walls, as the elephant house was used as a prison cell in 1278.

The chapels were not neglected, and provision was made to pay the Chaplain 50s a year plus vestments and communion plate. The Chapel of St John was painted and refurbished to include stained glass windows, which depicted the Virgin and Child, the Holy Trinity, and St John the Baptist. Major repairs were made to the Chapel of St Peter ad Vincula—it was re-roofed, fitted with glazed windows, re-plastered with lime, and generally re-decorated. We know that the Chapel was moved slightly to the south, probably by Henry III, because of the problem of building wall defences with the Chapel remaining in its original location. The major refurbishing may indicate that, as we suspect, the wall to the west of the Brick Tower was unfinished by Henry. There is a dearth of records of the later building phases, possibly because Henry's orders were delivered by word of mouth.

Henry III had serious clashes with the barons over his persistent breaching of one of the key provisions of Magna Carta by levying taxes without consultation. In 1234 there was a battle that the King lost, but the nobles did not exact penance from Henry other than promises from him to consult in future. His marriage with

*The Martin Tower, once the home of the Crown Jewels.*

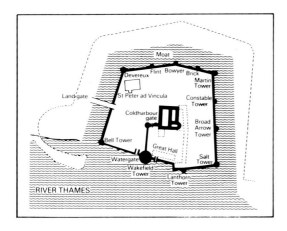

The Tower of London, c.1270.
The achievement of Henry III
leaps to the eye. The precinct has
been pushed out to the east to
match Bishop Longchamp's
extension to the west, so that the
White Tower and inner bailey are
now roughly in the centre of the
whole site. The walls are fortified
by a series of eleven towers
reinforced by a new moat. The
northern half of the original west
wall has gone; the southern half,
rebuilt, meets the river wall at the
Wakefield Tower which defends
the new water entrance. In the
west wall Henry built a grand
landgate, but this fell down before
the end of his reign and was later
rebuilt. The White Tower itself
and the inner bailey are defended
by the massive new Coldharbour
Gate. The Chapel of St Peter ad
Vincula is now within the Tower
walls. The site of the Menagerie is
not known; it would certainly
have been somewhere in the outer
bailey for ease of public access,
perhaps in the vicinity of the
landgate. Note that towers and
other features are given their
modern names.

Eleanor of Provence in 1236 diverted matters—she was a great success, being beautiful and of the same tastes as Henry. Unusually for those days, he was both devoted and faithful.

All went well until Henry once again ran short of money and borrowed heavily at exorbitant rates of interest. Fruitless expeditions to recover the French territories, lost by John, did not help and he had to seek help from the Council of Barons. Once again, he was full of promises which he did not mean to keep and eventually, expecting trouble he moved the Queen into the Tower. In 1263 the barons and the City of London laid siege to the Queen and her foreign mercenaries; she tried to escape by river but was pelted from London Bridge with rubbish and mud which she threw back at her assailants.

The barons led by Simon de Montfort defeated the King in battle at Lewes in Sussex in 1264. Both the King and Prince Edward were taken prisoner and Montfort ruled the country. Parliament was enlarged but Prince Edward, freed after Lewes, soon gathered together an army, defeated Montfort, who was killed in the battle, and reinstated his father to power. Henry punished the City by imprisoning its major officers, including the Mayor, and reserved the rents from the shops on London Bridge for the Queen. There was a final siege of the Tower by the Earl of Gloucester, the champion of the City of London, which might well have succeeded had it not been for the efforts of the Jews who

*The interior of the Martin Tower.*

had taken refuge there. Over many centuries, the Jewish community in the City had a 'love-hate' relationship with the Tower, as it was either their refuge or their prison, depending on the politics of the day. Gloucester's siege was defeated by the arrival of Henry's troops and London was again under the menace of the Tower.

There were two Tower prisoners of note during Henry's reign, the first being Hubert de Burgh in 1232, already mentioned. The second was Gruffyd, son of Llywelyn the Great, who ruled North Wales. Llywelyn took advantage of Henry's preoccupation with the barons to expand his territories. Gruffyd was captured and put in the Tower, where he tried to emulate Flambard's feat of escaping by rope from the upper apartments of the White Tower. The rope was a makeshift affair and Gruffyd was just as big and fat as Flambard; the rope broke and Gruffyd's head was driven into his breastbone between the shoulders—a ghastly sight.

Henry III ended his reign peacefully in 1272 having governed with the support of Parliament since the death of Montfort. He was succeeded by his son Edward I (1272–1307) who took the throne at the age of thirty-three.

He towered over his contemporaries who gave him the nickname of 'Longshanks'. He was tough, fearless, an expert tournament fighter, an outstanding general, and the best European expert on castle construction of the time, particularly in relation to the new weapons available—the great siege engines, such as the mangonel and trebuchet. The latter was capable of throwing extremely heavy missiles into fortresses making defence in depth essential. Under Edward I the Tower was therefore transformed into a concentric fortress (a central keep encircled by, at least, two rings of defences) and Edward was determined to build quickly. He never forgot the humiliation suffered by his father, Henry III, when defeated by Simon de Montfort, and was determined that neither the barons nor the City of London would ever repeat their victories. He was aware of the power of the City which had increased fourfold in size since

the time of William the Conqueror, now numbering some 80,000 inhabitants. Edward was widely respected and feared by the barons who took heed of his quick revenge on Montfort, whom he had defeated and killed within months of Henry's surrender at Lewes. A measure of their respect is that no one thought of taking advantage of his two years' absence from England after his father's death—he was recovering from a wound suffered in the Holy Land at Acre. He married Eleanor of Castille when he was fifteen years of age and was a truly devoted husband. The original cross at Charing Cross was one of those built at every resting place between Nottingham and London when, some thirty-six years later, he escorted her body to Westminster. His second wife was Margaret, daughter of Philip III of France.

His work in the Tower started in 1275 and took only ten years to complete—men and money were no object. He started by employing Master Robert of Beverley to repair the damage from previous sieges, then continued to finish off the western wall left uncompleted by his father Henry III. At the same time he spent six years in completing a new, and much larger, moat under the expert guidance of Master Walter of Flanders. The Beauchamp Tower replaced the existing landgate of 1240, and Edward made an entirely new land entrance to the Tower consisting of the Lion Gate (giving access to a drawbridge), a barbican (the Lion Tower), the Middle Tower with its double portcullis, and the Byward Tower with yet another double portcullis—all this to reach the Outer Ward which housed only soldiers, servants, and the less important persons of the Royal Household. The Inner Ward was guarded by the portcullis of the Bloody Tower arch.

On the waterfront, land was reclaimed and the great water entrance was built (later named Traitors' Gate but originally known as the Water Gate). This was guarded by the massive St Thomas's Tower, which became the sleeping quarters of the King, and was joined by an arch to the Wakefield Tower, then used for reception rooms. As always, the guard were on the lower

*The Middle Tower. This was once in the 'middle' of the western entrance, linked to the Byward Tower on the inner side of the Moat and the now destroyed Lion Tower on the outer side. It is defended by a drawbridge and double portcullis, and is the main visitors' entrance today.*

floor, to dominate the entrance, and the arrow slits show their action stations. In the King's apartments were stained glass windows and off his bedroom was a small oratory dedicated to Thomas Becket, presumably to appease Becket's ghost which had seemed so destructive in 1240. Traitors' Gate is an arch without a keystone (there is room for two London double-decker buses to park under it) and no one wanted this to fall down. St Thomas's Tower was used by Edward I and II, and by Edward III until he moved to more comfortable quarters near the Lanthorn Tower. It was the home of distinguished guests, then distinguished prisoners, until in the eighteenth century it became first, a hospital, then a water-mill and administrative offices. In 1869 it was refurbished for the Keeper of the Jewel House and the arch, which had been removed at the time of Charles II, was replaced to give him access to the Crown Jewels which had been moved to the Wakefield Tower opposite. Sir Walter Ralegh is said to have married Elizabeth Throckmorton in the Oratory and as I live in St Thomas's I can vouch for the ghost. My wife has always been disappointed that the ghost was not Sir Walter Ralegh (after all, he was an attractive man and his bailiff in Devon was named Meares) but we know our apparition to be not Becket but an old Abbot, very concerned with the Oratory. In more modern times Sir Roger Casement was imprisoned here before his execution at Pentonville in August 1916.

To the east from St Thomas's came the Well and Develin Towers; thence the wall ran north and then west to form the concentric castle. More compensation had to be paid to St Katharine's as the new Moat required the demolition of many dwellings. The City was not best pleased and looked at the Tower with some trepidation.

There were private entrances for the King's personal use just to the east of the Byward Tower and also to the east of St Thomas's Tower in line with the old private watergate beside the Wakefield Tower. The top storey was added on to the Bloody Tower, transforming it from the gatehouse of Henry III and, to complete the

*The modernised interior of St Thomas's Tower, the author's home.*

*The White Tower by night. In the foreground are the eighteenth-century houses now occupied by the Tower chaplain and doctor.*

(Above) *On the roof of the White Tower*

(Right) *The south-east corner of the White Tower, showing the windows of the curved apse of St John's Chapel*

picture, there were bastions where the gun emplacements of Brass Mount and Legge's Mount are now located. The whole amounted to a massive concentric fortress, particularly when the moat was filled with water some 20 feet (6 m) deep, reaching to the level of the grass today.

Edward did not neglect the palace, although clearly his priority was defence. Work took place in the Great Hall, the Small Hall, and the King and Queen's gardens, and there is mention of the Queen's Chapel, which was probably in the buildings running south from the White Tower. In 1286 he completely rebuilt the Chapel of St Peter ad Vincula.

Even while the building works were in progress, Edward was putting the enlarged accommodation available to full use. In 1278, Jews from all over England, accused of clipping the coinage, were brought to the Tower—even the old elephant house had to be used. At about this time the Mint moved from the City of London into the Tower where it remained until 1807, moving then to the Minories over a period of five years. (It remained there until the 1950s when the presses were installed in Wales.)

It was probably in Edward I's reign that some of the earliest public records were first kept at the Tower. These were the parchment rolls and documents recording the work of the lawcourts and government departments. Soon the Tower became the main Public Record Office and remained so until the mid-nineteenth century, the ever-growing volume of records eventually occupying the Wakefield Tower and a large part of the White Tower.

Travelling was a way of life for Edward I. He was determined to revise the laws of England and see for himself the problems that had to be solved. Much of our legal fabric today is based on statutes that were issued by him and our jury system evolved from the developments and expansion of his day; not for nothing was he also known as the 'Lawmaker'. Apart from his legal and soldierly qualities, Edward had a rough sense of humour but his was not an endearing personality.

His ambitions caused problems with the Welsh and Scots whose remote areas were only nominally under the control of the central government. Llywelyn, the Prince of Wales, had been betrothed to Simon de Montfort's daughter during her father's ascendancy—this was too much for Edward who brought Llywelyn to book after a series of fierce battles. Despite promises of good behaviour, Llywelyn went back on his word, and was eventually killed; his head was sent to Edward who ordered it to be crowned with ivy and paraded through the streets of London. It ended on a pike on the White Tower. In 1301, Edward gave the title of Prince of Wales to his eldest son, the future Edward II who had been born in Caernarvon in 1284 and was known as Edward of Caernarvon. This is the origin of the present custom for the heir to the Throne to be given this title.

The Scots proved difficult to control, particularly when John Baliol, King of Scotland, allied himself with France in 1296 and marched southwards. He ended as a prisoner in the Salt Tower, where he spent two years—yet another man defeated by Edward's battle craft. Though he did not succeed in subduing the Scots, Edward marched far into Scotland and captured the Stone of Scone as well as the Stuart Sapphire. This sapphire is in the back of the present Imperial State Crown (it was in the front for Queen Victoria, but was moved to make way for the Second Star of Africa in 1911) and has an interesting history. In 1214 it was in the hands of Alexander II of Scotland, Edward I appropriated it, Edward III returned it to David II of Scotland who gave it to his sister, Margery Bruce; she married Walter the Steward, and the stone remained with the Stuart family until 1807 when the last of the Stuarts, Cardinal York (Henry IX) died, leaving the sapphire to George III. It came to him by somewhat devious means and has stayed with the Crown Jewels to this day.

William Wallace was the next Scottish problem and Edward had to return from battles in France to deal with him. Wallace was finally betrayed in 1305 and was hanged, drawn, and quartered. Robert Bruce was crowned King at Scone, but Edward was unable to meet this challenge as he was then towards the end of his life; it had to be left to his son to take action against Bruce. Edward's wars with the Welsh and Scots required careful planning and preparation, and the accumulation of great stores of armour and weapons. From this time, the Tower of London became the centre of military administration and the national arsenal, as it was to be until Queen Victoria's reign.

The 'Crown Jewels' are always a sensitive subject and so it proved in 1303 when Richard de Podlicote succeeded in stealing them from the crypt of Westminster Abbey. He spent ninety-eight days tunnelling through walls 13 feet (4 m) thick to reach the royal treasury, and on 25 April 1303 he succeeded. He had accomplices both within and without the Abbey and soon gold and silver cups and plate found their way into almost every goldsmith's window in London. It was too good to last and by 25 June Richard and his mistress Joan Pycard were arrested, together with forty-eight monks, and to the Tower they went. There was a complicated trial and in March 1304 William Palmer, the Keeper of Westminster Palace, and four laymen were hanged while the monks, after much lobbying, were set free. Podlicote himself was hanged in 1306, and his skin was stretched across the door of the Chapel of the Pyx as a warning to others. The Pyx is an oak chest where, traditionally are held the gold and silver master coins used to check the newly minted output for weight and accuracy of design. The Chapel of the Pyx was a treasury holding the Crown Jewels which, after this theft, were moved to the Tower. The entrance to the Chapel is on the East Cloister Walk at Westminster Abbey and it contains the oldest stone altar there. St Edward's relics remained in the

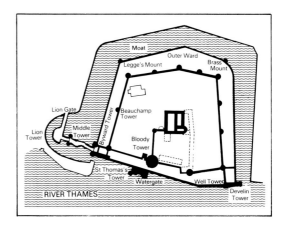

The Tower of London, c. 1300. *The Tower has reached its final shape with the building work of Edward I. Henry III's moat has been filled in and replaced by another, both broader and deeper, defended by a new external wall strengthened at the northwest and northeast corners by bastions later replaced by Legge's Mount and Brass Mount. The Beauchamp Tower replaces the old, collapsed landgate in the inner wall, and a formidable new land entrance has been built in the southwest corner; this is the entrance used by visitors today. The southeastern corner of the Moat is defended by the Develin Tower, later bridged to the Iron Gate on the opposite bank. The river frontage has been reinforced by a new external wall and the building of St Thomas's Tower with the Watergate (later known as Traitors' Gate) beneath. The Bloody Tower has been built over the old watergate. The new outer ward between the two walls was probably the first home of the Mint inside the Tower (the southwest area of the outer ward has been known as Mint Street for many centuries) and of other administrative buildings, erected and demolished as the need arose. The Lion Tower (Barbican) later held the Menagerie but the date of this move is not known; at some stage the Menagerie seems to have been housed by the river, probably on the site of the Lion Tower.*

Abbey until the execution of Charles I in 1649. They included the coronation crowns but details of other items are not precisely known; the term 'Crown Jewels' is very general and includes church and banqueting plate.

Just before he died, Edward made the first move against pollution in the Tower—a problem which has persisted over the centuries. He banned the production of bricks in the vicinity of the Tower, as long as Queen Margaret was in residence, because of the 'infection and corruption of the air by such burning of kilns'.

Edward I was buried in Westminster Abbey on 27 October 1307; he had completed the concentric Tower in some 18 acres of land, a palace and fortress surrounded by two separate circles of towers and battlements, the whole encompassed by a formidable moat. On his tomb are the words *Pactum serva* (Keep troth) and *Scotorum malleus* (Hammer of the Scots). His last instruction was that his bones were to be carried at the head of the English army until every Scot had surrendered. A fighter to the end!

# II
# *The Middle Period*
## 1307–1485

Edward II (1307–27) was similar in physique to Edward I; they were both powerfully built and immensely tall. Otherwise, the first English Prince of Wales proved to be weak, effeminate and immature, a stark contrast to the strong character of his father. He was obsessed with his favourites, first Piers Gaveston, a handsome young Frenchman, then Hugh Despenser; both were executed by the barons: Gaveston by the axe, Despenser hanged '50 feet high'. Edward married Isabella, daughter of the King of France, a union that proved to be his ultimate downfall; he was to pay dearly for neglecting his wife who was a strong character, a beauty, and highly popular with the citizens of London. She bore a healthy heir to the throne, Prince Edward, in 1312; there were three further children, the youngest was always known as Joanna, or Joan, of the Tower because she was born there. She was betrothed to Prince David of Scotland at the early age of five and later became his Queen.

The reign started badly as the King infuriated the barons by his reliance on his favourites and by his disregard for the terms of Magna Carta; they took their revenge by summarily beheading Gaveston in June 1312 in circumstances more akin to murder than judicial trial.

On 24 June 1314 the English army was thrashed by Robert Bruce at the battle of Bannockburn; Edward even managed to lose the Regalia in this débâcle. He regained his confidence, however, from a successful storming of

*The Wharf and the river wall, with the Lanthorn Tower and the White Tower turrets emerging from the trees.*

Leeds Castle after Lady Badlesmere, the wife of the owner, had insulted the Queen by refusing her hospitality for the night and, adding injury to insult, set her archers to work, killing some members of the Queen's retinue. Lady Badlesmere was sent to the Tower and had the doubtful honour of being the first woman prisoner of note in that forbidding fortress. A more formidable prisoner was Roger Mortimer, one of the most dangerous of the barons. He escaped to France in 1323 and two years later was joined by Queen Isabella, now alienated from her husband. Mortimer and Isabella became lovers.

The Queen had Prince Edward with her and the heir to the throne proved to be a trump card against her husband. In 1326 she marshalled an army and, supported by Mortimer, defeated the King who was then incarcerated in Kenilworth Castle and forced to abdicate in favour of his son. He had not long to live as he was removed to Berkeley Castle where he was kept in disgraceful circumstances, treated as a madman, and, in September 1327, brutally murdered. A chronicler of the day said that his intestines were burnt out by the insertion of a white-hot iron bar through a horn funnel to prevent the body showing marks. Such was this medieval, brutal, age where men and women enjoyed the sight of offenders being disembowelled, branded, having hands or ears cut off, or being burnt at the stake.

Under Edward II the Tower was neglected and the royal apartments fell into a state of

43

*The east drawbridge and Cradle Tower, with St Thomas's Tower behind.*

disrepair, though in 1322, after complaints by Queen Isabella who had just given birth to her daughter there, the Constable was dismissed and repairs put in hand. Perhaps the most major change was the strengthening of the Outer Wall between St Thomas's Tower and the Develin Tower, combined with the crenellating and repair of the Martin, Constable, Broad Arrow, and Salt Towers. A new gate was constructed for the water entrance, St Thomas's Tower, and additional missile-throwing artillery, resembling giant crossbows, was installed along the eastern walls. The Menagerie was probably in the area of the Lion Tower, the barbican built by Edward I as part of the outer defences, and the Keeper of the King's Lions and Leopards had become a regular appointment. It was left to Edward III to make the next real impact on the structure of the Tower.

Edward III (1327–77)—a king, truly gallant—was a successful monarch, renowned as being a worthy successor to the legendary King Arthur and his Round Table. He was good-looking, shrewd, a strong character, a man fond of the arts and an excellent soldier. His reign started inauspiciously, when he was only fifteen, under the domination of Roger Mortimer but, once eighteen, he threw off the yoke, having Mortimer imprisoned in the Tower and then hanged, drawn and quartered at Tyburn. He married Philippa of Hainault in 1328 (this was part and parcel of the deal made by his mother, Queen Isabella, for French support in overthrowing Edward II). For an arranged marriage it was spectacularly successful. Edward and Philippa transformed the palace buildings within the Tower, where they lived for much of their reign. Work in the Tower started with the extension of the Wharf eastwards, as far as the watergate at St Thomas's Tower. Then followed the construction and, in places, repair of palace buildings which stretched south from the Wardrobe Tower to the Lanthorn, and thence west, via the Great Hall, to the Wakefield. The King's apartments moved to either the Lanthorn, or to the east end of the Great Hall. Latrines were installed although baths were limited to mobile tubs. The

King and Queen are said to have bathed together in a large, deep, two-seater, oak tub once a month—togetherness was to conserve the hot water! Between 1348 and 1355 the Cradle Tower was built in the Outer Wall to give a private water entrance for the King, as the St Thomas's Tower entrance was often cluttered with small craft. A small boat could be lifted up in a cradle (hence 'Cradle Tower') and entrance gained for the King's guests away from the common herd; there were two portcullises for added protection. The Cradle Tower today has been much restored from its original construction. The Bloody Tower was also reconstructed with a new vaulted gateway and portcullis, the latter weighing two tons, and requiring thirty men to lift it. Many a Yeoman Warder has told the story of the film star Errol Flynn lifting the portcullis single-handed in one of his romantic films.

The King, ably supported by his eldest son the Black Prince, was a successful, although somewhat reluctant, warrior. His spectacular success at the battle of Crécy followed by the siege and capture of Calais in 1346 was emulated some ten years later by the Black Prince at Poitiers. It was in the latter battle that the ostrich feathers (now the Prince of Wales's feathers) were taken from the helmet of the blind King John of Bohemia who was killed in the fighting; he was afterwards honoured by Edward III who attended his funeral with the Black Prince. Also from Poitiers came a vast number of French prisoners to be lodged in the Tower, including the French King himself, John the Good. David II of Scotland, taken prisoner after the battle of Neville's Cross, was already in the Tower so there had to be some reshuffling of accommodation. Vast ransoms were claimed and paid; affluence reigned, in contrast to Edward's earlier poverty, when he had had to pawn his crown in France to pay his soldiers. (This is why, constitutionally, the crowns of England cannot leave the country—a repetition of Edward III's recourse to a pawn-broker could not be tolerated. George V bene-fited from this rule in 1911 as the Imperial State Crown was not allowed to leave England for the Delhi Durbar and the Imperial Crown of India, sometimes called the Durbar Crown, was made for him instead, using precious stones provided by the Maharajahs of India.)

It was an exciting reign. In 1348 the King created the Order of the Garter. The story goes that he was dancing with his cousin the Countess of Salisbury (also known as Joan, the fair maid of Kent), at a ball to celebrate the victory at Calais. Joan dropped her garter and was highly embarrassed but the King, gallant as ever, picked it up, pinned it to his left knee, and said to the giggling courtiers 'honi soit qui mal-y-pense' ('evil be to him who evil thinks'). He then instituted the Order of the Garter, the oldest Order in Europe, which has some twenty-six members. The story is attractive but clearly the King had been entertaining the idea of founding a knightly order for some time.

Joan of Kent had a very romantic history. She was first married to Sir Thomas Holland at the age of twelve, but this marriage was kept secret from the King and later annulled. Edward married her to the Earl of Salisbury, but Thomas Holland became a very rich man from ransoms paid by prisoners after Poitiers and was able to purchase an annulment of the Salisbury marriage and remarry Joan. Unfortunately he died shortly afterwards, but the Widow Holland (as she was called) married the Black Prince in 1361 and was the mother of Richard II. At the time of the Peasants' Revolt in 1381, she was still, at the age of fifty-one, sufficiently attractive for the peasants who invaded the Tower to try to kiss her in bed.

The Black Prince died in 1376. Apart from his martial exploits, he is also commemorated by the large balas ruby in the front of the Imperial State Crown—the Black Prince's Ruby, given to him by Pedro the Cruel, King of Castile, after the battle of Najera, when the Black Prince provided Pedro with a safe haven. It is not a true ruby but a semi-precious stone, a spinel, and is pierced in the Eastern manner so that it can be worn on a turban. The hole is now filled by a small ruby which is clearly visible at the top of the stone. It has always been considered lucky to have a large red stone in the Imperial State

Crown and in consequence the Black Prince's Ruby has been used by most of our monarchs.

Edward III died in 1377 at the age of sixty-five, a lonely old man who had taken Alice Perrers as his mistress after the death of his wife Philippa; she had been a lady-in-waiting to the Queen.

Once again, a minor was on the throne of England. Richard II (1377–99), son of the Black Prince and Joan of Kent, was often known as Richard of Bordeaux after the town of his birth. His coronation marked the first occasion when a king was to be escorted by his friends in procession from the Tower to Westminster Abbey, a custom followed by nearly all his successors for the next 300 years. The Regent was his uncle, John of Gaunt, eldest surviving son of Edward III, whose son Bolingbroke was later to become Henry IV. Richard was intelligent, spirited, brave, resourceful and a lover of the arts. Unfortunately, in his later years, he became wilful and dictatorial, a fault which led to his ultimate downfall.

A major event of his reign was the Peasants' Revolt in 1381 led by Wat Tyler. This was the culmination of much trouble between the peasants and their landlords, sparked off by the new poll-taxes imposed by Richard's ministers. As the peasant forces approached London Richard took refuge with the Court in the Tower. He addressed the crowd assembled on Tower Hill from one of the turrets and emerged to face the peasant army at Mile End. Meantime, a body of them was let into the Tower itself where, after looting and destruction, they murdered Simon Sudbury, who was Chancellor and Archbishop of Canterbury and the Treasurer Sir Robert Hales. These two had the doubtful distinction of establishing Tower Hill as a place of execution. The peasants could not find Richard's cousin Henry Bolingbroke, who was hidden by a loyal retainer. The following day the King had a further meeting with the malcontents in the course of which Wat Tyler was killed in a fracas with Mayor Walworth; Richard saved the day by his famous exhortation to the rebels, 'Sirs, will you shoot your King? I am your captain. I will be your leader. Let him who loves me follow me.' The peasants followed him, but he broke faith, having their leaders executed and the rest harried out of London.

In 1382, after years of conflict of interest with the City of London, an agreement was made which defined the bounds of the Tower; the Tower felt that the City buildings were too close to the walls and hampered the defence of the fortress whilst the City resented the Tower expanding and taking more land from them. Boundaries were to be inspected on Ascension Day by a procession consisting of the Constable of the Tower, his officers, freemen, and inhabitants of the Tower. This was the forerunner of the present ceremony of Beating the Bounds which takes place once every three years; the bounds are beaten by schoolboys who form part of the procession. In earlier times it was the boys who were beaten to impress the location on their young minds.

Richard did make some improvements to the Tower, apart from repairs required by the damage caused by the Peasants' Revolt, but these were limited. He extended the Wharf eastwards from St Thomas's, thus ending the use of the Cradle Tower as a watergate; this extension required the provision of a new entrance, a bridge and drawbridge between the Galleyman and Iron Gate Towers (no longer in existence). Hardly an improvement, but related to the Tower, was the first official execution on Tower Hill, that of Sir Simon Burley in 1387—over the years there were to be some 125 more as it was a splendid location for maximum publicity and drew huge crowds of spectators, sometimes as many as 20,000 people.

Conflict with the barons, particularly with his Lancastrian cousins, marked the latter period of Richard's reign and, after some two and a half years of virtual dictatorship—he had dissolved Parliament in 1398—the standard of revolt was raised by Henry Bolingbroke, who had been banished from England on flimsy pretexts in 1397. Richard was defeated, surrendering his throne to Henry. A few months later Richard was murdered in Pontefract Castle.

Henry IV (1399–1413) was an able king, who had a somewhat turbulent start and end to his reign. His health was poor and he died at the age of forty-six but his son, later to become Henry V, was more than able to support him in the later battles with the Welsh and Scots. Like most kings who win their thrones by force of arms, he found that the supporters of his predecessor remained a problem. Henry solved this by beheading all those he could lay hands on and there were many executions at Cirencester, Bristol and Oxford. Tower Hill was another popular site and before long there was a shortage of spikes on London Bridge for the display of the numerous heads.

There was no building work of note within the Tower but a major innovation was the first creation of Knights of the Bath at the Tower. Henry had a splendid procession from the Tower to Westminster Abbey for his coronation and on the preceding evening he gathered together forty-six knights in the White Tower for a ceremonial bath. Forty-six tubs were assembled, each magnificently canopied, and Henry, in procession with his priests, made the sign of the cross in water on the back of each knight. They then rested in forty-six beds, richly draped, before taking up their all-night vigil in the Chapel of St John. The end of the vigil was marked by each knight laying a penny and a taper on the altar—the penny for the King, the taper for God. This, in 1399, was the forerunner of the modern Order of the Bath.

The Tower kept up its record of famous prisoners by holding Prince James of Scotland, who became James I of Scotland while in captivity. The Prince, twelve years of age, had the misfortune to be captured by pirates in 1406 while on his way to France and was delivered to Henry in London. Two years in the Tower were followed by sixteen years in Nottingham Castle before he was finally ransomed. His father, King Robert, died of a broken heart—a truly sad story.

The next Henry, Henry V (1413–22), filled the Tower with French prisoners who, when ransomed, produced a better income for the State than do the visitors of today. 'Prince Hal' died young, at the age of thirty-four, but his

*Beating the Bounds. (From an old photograph in the Yeoman Warders Club.)*

famous victories at Harfleur and Agincourt have been enshrined in English history through the works of William Shakespeare. After Agincourt, many noble prisoners were brought back to the Tower, including the Duke of Orleans who spent the next twenty-five years living luxuriously in various English castles. Meanwhile, apart from maintenance, and the periodic draining and cleaning of the Moat, the fabric of the Tower remained unchanged. It had always housed an Armoury and warlike stores and these had been controlled by the Keeper of the Privy Wardrobe. In 1414 a new official, Nicholas Merbury, was appointed with the title of 'Master of the works of the King's engines and guns and of the ordnance'. Little is known of the detailed work undertaken by Masters of the Ordnance during the fifteenth century and they were not the only organisers of military equipment. Henry died in suspicious circumstances in France in August 1422—some thought he had been poisoned, but the cause is more likely to have been one of the many maladies caused by the insanitary conditions of the time.

Henry VI (1422–61) became King of England at the age of nine months—a few months later, on the death of his maternal grandfather Charles VI, he became King of France as well. Seldom could there have been anyone less suited for the task; he was pious, scholarly, gentle and kind, the attributes of a good monk, but lacked the fighting qualities of his father who was one of the strongest of the Plantagenet kings. The first half of the reign was disturbed by quarrels among the young King's uncles, the outcome being the loss of Henry's French possessions, with the exception of Calais. Henry also suffered from a streak of madness which first afflicted him in 1453. He was protected by his wife, Margaret of Anjou, a lady of ambition and courage, well suited to being the monarch herself. The effect on the Tower of Lancastrian ineptitude was to end the constant flow of French prisoners which had been the hallmark of Henry V's reign; the blunders of Henry's advisers were also to herald the beginning of the Wars of the Roses marked by the rise of the Duke of York and the putting down of Jack Cade's rebellion. The red rose of Lancaster is particularly familiar to me as it is the central part of the badge of the Intelligence Corps of which I was once Director. The story goes that when a band of Lancastrians dined together they would throw a red rose on the table which meant that they could speak freely—they were among friends. The Yorkists adopted a white rose—hence the name Wars of the Roses.

Henry played little part in government but, even at the age of seventeen, he had shown his interest in education by founding both Eton College and King's College Cambridge. On the anniversary of his murder on 21 May 1471, the Ceremony of the Lilies and Roses takes place in the Wakefield Tower. This consists of a short service attended by the Master of Eton and the Provost of King's College Cambridge, who lay lilies and roses respectively. These should be ceremonially burnt by the Keeper of the Jewel House but in these more worldly days they tend to be put to better use.

Henry was not idle about looking after the Tower as it was one of the places that gave him the seclusion he desired; mostly, however, his alterations were to the palace where he improved the windows and apartments. New kitchens, a new residence for the Keeper of the Lions, and a new drawbridge, were his other additions. In 1436, there was a disaster in the menagerie

*Lilies and roses. The annual ceremony in the Wakefield Tower, commemorating the murder of Henry VI.*

where an epidemic seems to have killed all the animals but they were quickly replaced; the post of 'Keeper of the King's Lions and Leopards' became titular, given to favourites of the monarch, and the care of the animals was delegated to secondary officials.

After 1455 there was a period of uneasy truce, followed by some savage battles which ended with a victory in 1461 by Edward, Duke of York; this secured him the throne, Henry and Margaret taking refuge with the Scots. The House of York was in ascendance.

Edward IV (1461–83) was an outstanding military leader with an eye for pretty women. He strengthened the garrison in the Tower, and declared all supporters of Henry to be guilty of high treason. Queen Margaret, that lady of steel, was undeterred and rallied her forces once again, but she was defeated in 1464, Henry being captured at Clitheroe, in Lancashire, and brought to the Tower in circumstances of humiliation and ridicule. He remained there for five years until the Earl of Warwick (the 'Kingmaker'), the King's cousin, managed to bring him back to the throne. This renewed reign lasted for some six months, but Edward was soon back, defeating the Lancastrians and killing Warwick at the battle of Barnet in 1471. Henry had to die. On 21 May 1471 Edward made a triumphal return to London and on the same evening Henry VI was murdered in the Oratory in the Wakefield Tower. It is said that he was stabbed while at his devotions, possibly by Richard of Gloucester, Edward's younger brother, later to become Richard III. Examination of Henry's remains in the nineteenth century revealed that he had a fractured skull so he may have been killed by a blow to the head.

Edward died in 1483, at the age of forty, he had earlier, in 1478, had his brother the Duke of Clarence condemned for treason by Parliament and privately executed in the Bowyer Tower— legend states that he was drowned in a butt of malmsey wine.

Richard III (1483–85) was no better or worse than many of his contemporaries—these were rough times, when the death of an individual was

of little account. Shakespeare made Richard into the arch-fiend of medieval times but in reality most strong kings behaved much as he did—they had little option if they were to survive. Richard seized the throne after being appointed Protector to his twelve-year-old nephew, the uncrowned Edward V. The boy was put in the Tower, to be joined later by his younger brother, after the summary execution of Lord Hastings, the strongest supporter of the young King. On Friday 13 June 1483 Richard manufactured a quarrel with Hastings in the Council Chamber of the White Tower saying, 'I will not eat my supper tonight until your head is off your shoulders'— the men-at-arms rushed in and dragged Hastings out to the vicinity of the Chapel of St Peter ad Vincula where he was beheaded, the block being a piece of wood left by a carpenter doing some repairs. Twenty-three days later, on 6 July, Richard of Gloucester was crowned Richard III.

The story of the two princes, as described by Sir Thomas More, has been hotly disputed and, indeed, cannot be proved or disproved. They were not seen after July 1483 and their deaths were thought to have occurred between 7 and 14 August. Some two hundred years later, during the reign of Charles II, the skeletons of two boys were found in rubble under the staircase leading to the Chapel of St John in the White Tower. Both then, and on re-examination in 1933, these bones were judged to be of the right age and size for the two Princes. They were interred by Charles II in an urn in Westminster Abbey where they remain to this day.

Sir Thomas More stated that Sir James Tyrell, said to be an emissary of Richard III, produced a warrant to the Tower Governor, Sir Robert Brackenbury, demanding the keys to the Bloody Tower where the princes were held. One of the guards, Miles Forrest, and Tyrell's groom John Dighton smothered the two boys and buried them in a corner of the Wakefield Tower. They were later re-buried by a young priest 'in consecrated ground'—the staircase leading to the Chapel of St John being as close as he could get to a consecrated area.

All the evidence came from supporters of Henry VII who would wish to denigrate Richard III, but the princes certainly disappeared from the Tower and Sir Thomas More had no other evidence. It need not have been Richard who authorised the killings but it seems unlikely that he would not have known the facts after the event. A famous mystery, but not out of character with the times.

Despite being a good and wise administrator, Richard could not gain the confidence of the people, and the ambitious adventurer Henry Tudor was ever on the horizon. Buckingham, Richard's friend, changed sides but was betrayed and beheaded; this only delayed the inevitable. Henry marshalled his forces in Harfleur, crossed the Channel, and on 22 August 1485 defeated Richard at the battle of Bosworth; Richard was abandoned in the field by his chief supporters, the Earl of Northumberland and Lord Stanley. The King was killed, fighting to the end, and his crown was placed on the head of Henry Tudor.

# III
# *The Bloody Years*
# 1485–1660

Henry VII (1485–1509) came to the throne in dramatic fashion and established the somewhat dictatorial style that was the hallmark of his reign. He married Elizabeth of York, daughter of Edward IV, in January of 1486, finally ending the 'Roses' era, and combined the red rose of Lancaster with the white rose of York to form the Tudor rose. He consolidated his position by eliminating any possible contenders for the throne and gave short shrift to the two pretenders, Lambert Simnel and Perkin Warbeck, both of whom claimed to be the younger of the two missing princes (i.e. the Duke of York). Simnel, the tool of more powerful conspirators, was sent to work in the royal scullery, and Warbeck was hanged. The princes' young cousin the Earl of Warwick, another possible threat, was beheaded in 1499.

Apart from its prison function, Henry kept the Tower busy. The Royal Ordnance continually expanded, manufacturing armaments on a large scale. It competed for space with the Mint which was given the task of reorganising the currency of the realm. By 1495 the Ordnance had at least one building of its own, probably located on the north side of the inner wall. The area between the inner and outer walls was referred to as the Mint although, in common with the Ordnance, little detail of the buildings is known until the seventeenth century.

There have always been Warders in the Tower, but the first mention of the Yeoman

*The White Tower at sunset.*

Body (popularly known as 'Beefeaters') originated with Henry VII. An old Tower record reads: 'On the 22nd day of August 1485 Henry, Earl of Richmond, was by public acclamation saluted on the Battle field of Bosworth King over England and was crowned on the 30th of October following. In the first year of his reign, the Yeoman of the Guard was first ordered of which the Yeoman Waiters or Warders of the Tower hath the seniority.' Henry VIII left twelve members of the Yeomen of the Guard in the Tower when he left for his coronation, the remainder staying with him as his personal bodyguard, but it was not until 1550 that their successors were appointed by Edward VI, at the behest of the Duke of Somerset, as 'Extraordinary members of the Yeomen of the Guard'; this was in recognition of the kind treatment given to the Duke while he was incarcerated in the Tower. Their historic duties were to guard the prisoners and attend the gates. Hence the Gentleman Gaoler looked after the prisoners' welfare and the Gentleman Porter organised the guard duties (to this day known as the 'Wait'); the latter was the senior. In full dress the Yeomen of the Guard can be distinguished from the Yeoman Warders by a gold crossbelt for an arquebus (a form of musket); the Yeoman Warders carry a partizan (a form of pike). The 'blue undress' uniform worn by the Yeoman Warders on most days of the year is a Victorian compromise as it was far too expensive to wear the

*Yeoman Warder Ramshall in state
dress.*

*(Right) Chief Yeoman Warder
Harding and Yeoman Gaoler
Maher (with ceremonial axe).*

*Sir Thomas More's cell in the lower Bell Tower.*

scarlet for everyday use. The term Beefeater is of unknown origin but may be a derogatory term stemming from the enormous rations of beef given to the Yeomen of the Guard and the Yeoman Warders in the days of Charles II. The number of Yeoman Warders rose to thirty-nine within thirty years of their inception and has varied little since, being forty-two in 1988. There are now three senior posts which are the Chief Yeoman Warder, the Yeoman Gaoler, and the Yeoman Clerk.

In 1501 Henry arranged the marriage of Catherine of Aragon to his eldest son, Arthur, who died some five months later. Consequently, to maintain the link with Spain, he betrothed her to his second son (later Henry VIII) but the marriage did not take place until seven years later, after he had succeeded to the throne at the age of eighteen. Henry VII died in 1509, having laid the foundations for the Tudor dynasty.

Henry VIII (1509–47) took full advantage of his father's consolidation of power as, by now, there were no serious rivals or, indeed, opposition to the sovereign. Henry loved women, hunting and the arts and, in his younger days, he was endowed with a strong physique matched only by his musical and scholastic talents. Unfortunately, an accident while jousting started his leg ulcer which led to his eventual deterioration in health, undoubtedly affecting his temper and judgement. His reign was dominated by his desire for a male heir and, apart from his succession of wives, this resulted in his quarrel with the papacy and the severance of the Church of England from the Church of Rome.

The Tower became notorious as a prison for those out of favour with Henry and, more often than not, they ended on the execution site at Tower Hill.

The Tower was not a common prison but a man of substance, convicted of treason, could expect to be transported there from Westminster by river (much safer than the narrow streets of London where rescue attempts might be made), the Yeoman Gaoler escorting him with the blade of the ceremonial axe towards him—a sign of a verdict of Guilty. He would enter the Tower by

the watergate (now called Traitors' Gate) and be held until the day appointed for the execution, when he would be handed over to the City authorities. A few executions took place within the Tower itself, on the Green, notably in this reign those of Queen Anne Boleyn, Queen Catherine Howard together with Jane, Viscountess Rochford (lady-in-waiting to both Queens), and Margaret, Countess of Salisbury, the senior remaining member of the Pole branch of the Yorkist family. The latter was executed because, apart from being a troublemaker herself, her son, Cardinal Reginald Pole, who was in exile, opposed Henry's divorce and subsequent severance of the English Church from Rome; Henry could not get at the son so executed his mother. It is said that she refused to lay her head on the block and was chased by the executioner striking her as and when he could. In all, there were six executions (seven, if Lord Hastings is included) in the Tower, the last being Robert Devereux, the Earl of Essex, in 1601. His was the result of special pleading but the others were in deference to their rank, sex, or closeness to the throne; Lady Jane Grey was the fifth lady.

As a method of execution, the axe was a privilege of the upper class, even though it sometimes took as many as five blows to sever the head. The alternative was horrific; the sentence pronounced on Sir Walter Ralegh in 1603 is typical (in the event, in 1618, he was given the privilege of the axe). It read:

> You shall be led from hence to the place whence you came, there to remain until the day of execution. And from thence you shall be drawn on a hurdle through the open streets to the place of execution, there to be hanged and cut down alive, and your body shall be opened, your heart and bowels plucked out, and your privy members cut off and thrown into the fire before your eyes. Then your head to be stricken off from your body and your body shall be divided into four quarters, to be disposed of at the King's pleasure. And God have mercy on your soul.

Anne Boleyn made a special plea to Henry to be executed in the French style—by the sword. This postponed her execution by one day, as the executioner from Calais was delayed by bad weather, but it was a wise request as the sword is a much more accurate weapon than the axe. She died on Tower Green on 19 May 1536 and, to this day, roses are placed on her burial site in St Peter ad Vincula by an anonymous society.

Henry had both the defences and the palace at the Tower renovated and repaired and he rebuilt Queen's House adjoining the Bell Tower. He also rebuilt St Peter ad Vincula, after a fire in 1512. The White Tower and some other towers were strengthened to take cannon, and both cannons and armour were made or stored in large quantities by the Royal Armouries. There is evidence that the Master of the Ordnance lived in the Brick Tower and that either the Bowyer or the Flint Tower was used for storage. In 1526 Mint Street had to be cleared of ordnance and cannon to give better access to the Mint workshops and, in the latter part of Henry's reign, the Mint came under great pressure, probably caused by successive debasements of the currency. A sub-mint was even opened at Southwark but this was short-lived.

Henry's reign started, as it was to continue, with executions. Edmund Dudley and Sir Richard Empson, Henry VII's financial advisers, became an embarrassment and were sacrificed to appease the people. Thomas Wolsey, the son of a butcher in Ipswich, ruled England for fourteen years but fell foul of Anne Boleyn and was only saved from the scaffold by dying en route to the Tower in 1529. He failed to engineer Henry's divorce from Catherine of Aragon who was no longer of an age to bear a son; her daughter was to become Mary I (Bloody Mary). Thomas Cromwell, a protégé of Wolsey, some eleven years later, followed his master, albeit in a more spectacular manner—he died on the scaffold.

After Henry's marriage to Anne Boleyn in 1533, a daughter was born (Elizabeth I), and the Act of Supremacy, creating Henry head of the English Church, was signed in 1534. Anne, a strongwilled and sharp tongued woman, was accused of adultery, and also of incest with her brother George, Viscount Rochford; furthermore she had failed to produce a male heir. Her end was inevitable, although the charges brought against her were exaggerated if not false, and she spent her last days in a room in Queen's House where she could see her scaffold being built, also the headless body of her brother being brought for burial at St Peter ad Vincula. Queen's House is not named after Anne Boleyn—if a king were on the throne it would be called King's House. It has always been the home of the Resident Governor and when this was the Lieutenant of the Tower it was referred to as the Lieutenant's Lodgings. Its present name dates from 1858 when the Major of the Tower became Resident Governor. A little earlier, Sir Thomas More, Wolsey's successor, had been held in the Lower Bell Tower for refusing to acknowledge Henry as head of the English Church, and John Fisher, Bishop of Rochester, was put in the Upper Bell for the same reason. This episode ended when the Pope unwisely promoted Fisher to Cardinal; Henry lost his temper and said, 'Before the hat reaches him, he shall have no head upon which to place it'. Fisher was executed on 22 June 1535 and More some two weeks later on 6 July. More's head was rescued, after six days' exposure on a spike on London Bridge, by his daughter Margaret Roper, who took it to the Roper family tomb in St Dunstan's at Canterbury.

Jane Seymour was the third of Henry's wives and this was his happiest marriage, though of short duration, Jane providing him in 1537 with a male heir to the throne (Edward VI) but dying in so doing. Henry's next wife, the unattractive Anne of Cleves (the Flanders Mare), was the undoing of Thomas Cromwell, who had proposed the match—Henry could not forgive him for this. Another divorce ensued followed by a marriage to Catherine Howard, a flighty lady who met her end on Tower Green on 13 February 1542 after being queen for only eighteen months—once her infidelities became known to the King his response was savage. Henry's last wife, Catherine Parr, outlived him and provided him with good nursing to his end in

The Queen's House. This is the
titular Tower residence of the
sovereign (and therefore known as
the King's House when a king is
on the throne). In practice it is the
home of the Resident Governor.
Until the reign of Queen Victoria
it was known as the Lieutenant's
Lodgings.

The room in the Queen's House
where Anne Boleyn is reputed to
have spent her last days.

1547; she had already nursed two ageing husbands to their deaths.

There were many executions throughout this bloody reign and also torture. Torture could be applied only by warrant of the King or the Privy Council and it was rare indeed for anyone above the rank of yeoman to suffer. There is little doubt, however, that the system was abused and men were not squeamish in their methods. Torture instruments were mobile and could be taken to the prisoner in his cell. The favourite

*The scold's bridle. This instrument of correction is on display in the Bowyer Tower.*

*The Scavenger's Daughter. This instrument of torture was introduced by Sir Leonard Skeffington in 1534. It was unique to the Tower.*

instrument of the time was the rack (the Duke of Exeter's daughter) but mention is also made of the 'Scavenger's daughter', which compressed the body, and the practice of hanging prisoners by their manacled wrists for long periods. Torture was not declared illegal until 1628. Anne Askew, a friend of Catherine Parr's, was a terrible victim of the rack, being stretched unmercifully, before eventually being burnt at the stake at Smithfield. She was suspected of trying to convert Catherine Parr to her extreme

Protestant view. Henry, despite his anti-papal moves, still considered himself a Catholic and would have reacted murderously if he thought that his wife did not hold the same beliefs.

Henry was the last of our kings to make much use of the Tower as a royal residence, and, in his later years, he preferred Whitehall if he wanted to be in London. The Tower now reverted to being a prison, a storehouse and manufacturing place for arms and armour, and the home of the Mint, and the Royal Menagerie. It was used, occasionally, as a palace by subsequent monarchs but there was no longer the need for such a safe refuge and both Whitehall and Hampton Court were much more attractive. Henry died in January 1547—the most notorious and most powerful of English kings.

Edward VI (1547–53) was nearly ten years old when he came to the throne. He governed through a Protector, his uncle the Duke of Somerset, whose policy was to maintain the breach with Rome and make England a Protestant country. Somerset was not a strong character, more of an idealist than a ruler, and his brother Thomas Seymour soon plotted against him. Seymour married Henry VIII's widow Catherine Parr, and was said to have made indelicate advances to Princess Elizabeth, appearing half-clothed in her bedroom and romping with her. He was charged with treason and executed in 1549 but Somerset's triumph was short-lived as he fell out of favour and went to the block himself in 1552.

The role of Protector was then taken by John Dudley, the self-seeking Duke of Northumberland. Edward was suffering from tuberculosis and, clearly, did not have long to live. Northumberland's aim was to deny Mary the throne and put one of his own family in her place. His choice was the sixteen-year-old Lady Jane Grey, granddaughter of Henry VIII's youngest sister Mary. With her parent's help Northumberland persuaded her to marry his fourth son Lord Guildford Dudley and influenced Edward to alter the succession in her favour on the grounds that Mary, a staunch Roman Catholic, would undo all the progress made in converting the country

*This inscription in the Beauchamp Tower was carved by or for John Dudley during his imprisonment, with his father and four brothers, after their failed attempt to establish Lady Jane Grey on the throne.*

to the Protestant faith. Edward fell ill and died, in somewhat suspicious circumstances, on 6 July 1553; some thought his symptoms were more indicative of poison than tuberculosis and that his end had been hastened.

Lady Jane Grey was brought to the Tower and proclaimed Queen. It was all a fantasy, as Mary had no intention of abandoning her claim to the throne and marched on London with an army of 10,000 men, amid the acclaim of the population. The Dudleys were put in the Tower, the famous Dudley inscriptions in the Beauchamp Tower bear witness to this. The Duke of Northumberland was executed soon afterwards, but Lady Jane, her husband and her father remained in the Tower. Lady Jane was removed from the royal lodgings and held in No 5 Tower Green to downgrade her status, under the care of Mr Partridge, the Gentleman Gaoler. Mary had no initial intention of executing Jane or Guildford Dudley but unfortunately the Wyatt rebellion forced her hand. This rebellion was put down on 6 February 1554, and Lady Jane Grey was executed six days later, just short of her seventeenth birthday and immediately after her husband. It was a sad end to a beautiful and brave girl—the victim of a ruthlessly ambitious family. Her father, Henry Grey, the Duke of Suffolk, was also executed.

The rebellion by Sir Thomas Wyatt also caused Princess Elizabeth to be sent to the Tower as she was suspected of taking part in the plot. She must have thought that she was to follow in the footsteps of her mother Anne Boleyn but after two months she was released to Woodstock where she spent the next five years in comfortable circumstances though under virtual house arrest. While in the Tower she was accommodated in the Upper Bell, in a fair degree of comfort, dining with the Resident Governor in the evening. Her arrival, on the steps of Traitors' Gate, in the pouring rain, was dramatic. She declared: 'Here landeth as true a subject, being a prisoner, as ever landed at these steps, and before thee, O God, I speak it, having none other friends but thee.' She then refused to move until persuaded by the Lieutenant of the Tower.

Traitors' Gate

'Bloody Mary' proved to be as savage as her father towards anyone who did not bend to her will and, over the next five years, there were many executions and burnings, and much torture of prisoners. These mostly took place in locations other than the Tower. The victims included Thomas Cranmer, Archbishop of Canterbury, Nicholas Ridley, Bishop of London, and Hugh Latimer, Bishop of Worcester, all of whom were executed at Oxford although imprisoned in the Tower before trial.

The marriage of Mary to Philip of Spain was highly unpopular. There was a proxy marriage said to have taken place in the Chapel of St John but more probably in Whitehall, later followed

*The entrance to the Tower for Tudor prisoners of state, who were usually brought by water. This watergate is universally known as the 'Traitors' Gate'.*

by the actual ceremony at Winchester in July 1554. Despite Mary's pleas, Philip was rarely in England and she became a disillusioned woman, particularly as her military support for her husband brought about the loss of Calais—the last English possession on the Continent. She suffered from dropsy, and died in 1558.

Elizabeth I (1558–1603) was welcomed by all and she took the throne in a countrywide mood of euphoria. As was customary she went first to the Tower, where she spent a week before her coronation on 15 January 1559, but she did not use the palace again as she hated the memories it brought her. Though not a beauty, she had a

*A ghost of the past. The
steps of Traitors' Gate.*

*This astrological chart on the wall of the Salt Tower was carved by Hugh Draper, who was imprisoned there in 1560.*

commanding presence and was extremely clever, with a gift for languages. She always chose her advisers well and was adept at walking a political tightrope, using her potential in the marriage market as a weapon for political manœuvre. She did not set out to persecute Roman Catholics but her policy changed when plots were discovered against her, and in the latter part of her reign the hunt for Jesuits became fanatical. She always reacted badly towards the marriage of those close to her; this was one of her less attractive features.

Elizabeth's cousin Margaret Lady Lennox, the mother of Lord Darnley, was consigned to the Tower for her part in bringing about the marriage between her son and Mary Queen of Scots, which Elizabeth feared for dynastic reasons. She was held in Queen's House for some two years until she was released in 1567 after Darnley's murder. An inscription over the fireplace commemorates her imprisonment in what is still known as the Lennox room. The room itself is said to be haunted. The story goes that on a Thursday evening a strange scent can be detected and it is unwise for an unmarried woman to sleep there as she may be suffocated. Not knowing this legend, my wife and I spent a Thursday night in this room, and on awakening in the morning my wife exclaimed, 'I felt that I

was being suffocated during the night—and what is this strange smell?' Perhaps the legend should be respected!

Another to suffer Elizabeth's displeasure was Sir Walter Ralegh. He seduced, then married, Elizabeth Throckmorton, a lady-in-waiting to the Queen. Elizabeth could accept the seduction but not the marriage and Ralegh was sent to the Tower—this time, the Brick Tower—but she soon relented and Ralegh came back into favour.

Robert Devereux, Earl of Essex, was a young favourite of the ageing Queen; he became too arrogant and, foolishly, took part in an amateurish plot against her thereby signing his death warrant. The Tudors never mixed business with pleasure but for sentimental reasons Elizabeth heeded Devereux's pleas against public execution at Tower Hill and he was executed privately within the Tower.

The Tower did not change during the later years of Elizabeth's reign which saw the Armada defeated (1588), the execution of Mary Queen of Scots (1587), and the Virgin Queen unable to secure the succession—a Tudor failing. She did, however, ensure that James VI of Scotland would succeed her although she did not actually designate him. Queen Elizabeth died on 24 March 1603, having equalled 'Bloody Mary's' total of victims but in forty-five years rather than five.

The Tower was no longer wanted as a palace because monarchs preferred more comfortable residences in more attractive surroundings. Nevertheless it was a favourite resort of James I (1603–25) who loved to watch fights between lions and mastiffs in the Royal Menagerie. During his reign the Menagerie was further developed for both bull- and bear-baiting; the public must have been admitted, as in 1609 a child was killed by a bear.

James hated Ralegh and was delighted to have him convicted on a trumped-up charge of conspiring to put Arbella Stuart on the throne. Arbella was the next in line for both the Scottish and the English thrones, and had been prevented from marrying both by Elizabeth and James as they foresaw a threat to the succession if she

*A page from the baptismal register of the Chapel of St Peter ad Vincula showing the entry in 1607 for Carew, son of Sir Walter Ralegh.*

should have children. In 1609 she married William Seymour without the King's permission; she was held prisoner in Lambeth while he was sent to the Tower and lodged in St Thomas's Tower. They both escaped a year later but through some muddle took different ships to the Continent. Seymour succeeded but Arbella was overtaken by a frigate, brought back to England, and imprisoned, first in the Upper Bell Tower then later in the Lennox room where she became ill. She died of self-induced starvation in 1615, probably being insane at the time. Seymour returned to England and was pardoned; he then married the daughter of Robert Devereux, but on his death some years later his will contained the touching request that his body be buried alongside that of Arbella Stuart.

Ralegh was sentenced to death but this sentence was held in abeyance; he spent nearly thirteen years in the Bloody Tower where he wrote his famous 'History of the World'. James released him in 1616 to lead an expedition to Guiana but is said to have leaked his plans to the King of Spain who organised a hot reception for Ralegh. The expedition failed and Ralegh was sent to the Tower, still under his old sentence, and his execution followed a few days later on 29 October 1618 at Old Palace Yard, Westminster. Prince Henry, the Prince of Wales, might have saved him but he had died suddenly in 1615 (some say of poison) and Ralegh lost his only influential friend.

Guy Fawkes was interrogated in the Tower in 1605 after being discovered with barrels of gun-

The room in the Bloody Tower
where Sir Walter Ralegh wrote his
History of the World.

Sir Walter Ralegh's bedroom in
the Bloody Tower.

powder in the cellars below Parliament. He was put on the rack in the White Tower for two hours before being brought back to the Council Chamber in Queen's House where he made a full confession. In 1608 a memorial plaque was put in the Council Chamber describing the events and naming the conspirators.

Charles I (1625–49) was the second son of James I and held to the divine right of kings— this cost him his head. He was the first monarch not to visit the Tower once during his reign, and he ruled through the inner circle of his Court, using his chosen favourites. Inevitably, he was in conflict with Parliament and, although he protected his friend the Duke of Buckingham (assassinated by John Felton in 1628), he failed to prevent the executions of the Earl of Strafford (Black Tom) in 1641 and Archbishop Laud in 1645. Charles wanted to have Felton tortured in the Tower; this was declared illegal but Felton was hanged at Tyburn, despite his popularity, for having killed Buckingham.

Up to 1642 the Tower was still a showpiece for visiting dignitaries and was used as such by the Stuarts; subsequently this function was overtaken by the requirements for the prison population. The Civil War started in 1642; Parliament took over the Tower which became crammed with prisoners until the Restoration in 1660. There is an existing record which shows that prisoners were housed in the Cradle, Well, Salt, Broad Arrow, Constable, Martin, Beauchamp, Bell, Bloody, Wakefield and Lanthorn Towers. In January 1649 Charles I was executed at Whitehall, going to his death with considerable dignity.

Oliver Cromwell, Lord Protector from 1649 to 1658, had little effect on the Tower although he caused Parliament to appoint a Commission to dispose of the Crown Jewels and the Regalia. Much was melted down for coinage, jewels were sold. Only a few items survive, mostly bought by supporters of the monarchy or jewellers for stock. Cromwell died in 1658; his son Richard proved to be no effective successor and the Protectorate came to an end in May 1659. General George Monck, in 1660, forced the issue and invited Charles I's eldest son to take the throne as Charles II.

# IV
# *The Later Stuarts*
# 1660–1714

Charles II (1660–85) was a man who liked women and, although he thought himself ugly, he had considerable attraction for the ladies. He was a big man, with a dark lugubrious face, a long nose, and eyes that sparkled with humour. His political antennae were well developed and he could be devious in the extreme. The people of England welcomed him back with open arms and he took particular care not to indulge in a blood-bath of retribution against his father's enemies. This did not exclude the trial of the regicides closely connected with the death of his father, three of whom were Lieutenants (Resident Governors) of the Tower. These were Sir Isaac Pennington (died in 1660 while imprisoned in the Tower), Robert Tichborne (died in the Tower after twenty-seven years imprisonment), and Sir John Barkstead (hanged, drawn and quartered at Tyburn). Barkstead is of particular interest to me as his head was mounted on a pole and displayed over my home, St Thomas's Tower. He was also the cause of the famous Tower treasure hunt organised by Samuel Pepys. It was thought that Barkstead had concealed a large sum of money (£20,000 was mentioned) before his arrest, and Pepys's diaries contain a magnificent account of the frustrating search for the treasure. The excavations made were probably in the Lower Bell Tower. Some further exploration was done in modern times but no treasure was ever found.

Charles came to the throne a bachelor, albeit

*The Wharf, looking south-west from St Thomas's Tower. In days when much transport both of people and of freight was by river, and especially while the Ordnance was housed in the Tower, the Wharf was the scene of much activity. Nowadays royal salutes are fired from the gunpark at the western end.*

with many light-hearted attachments. He already had a son, James, by the comely Lucy Walters, who had spent six months in the Tower on her return to England from the Continent in 1656. She was released by Cromwell as, apart from being a mistress of Charles II when he was in exile, there was no reason to hold her. James, her seven-year-old son, was with her; he was later to become the Duke of Monmouth. The King's bachelor state was ended a year after the Restoration by his marriage to a charming Portuguese Princess, Catherine de Braganza, whom he dearly loved. Unfortunately they had no children but Charles fathered some thirteen acknowledged illegitimate children plus another eight of less certain parentage. (Some say that this is the reason why Queen Victoria commissioned a new royal christening font (the Lily Font), which is used by the Royal Family today; she was not going to have her children christened in the same font as Charles's bastards.) The names of some of his mistresses make splendid reading and include Frances Stuart ('la Belle Stuart', the Duchess of Richmond), Lady Castlemaine (the Duchess of Cleveland), Louise de Kérouaille (the Duchess of Portsmouth), and of course Nell Gwyn. The remarkable Charles managed to adore his wife, his mistresses, and his illegitimate children while, at the same time, they all adored him.

For his coronation, Charles went in procession from the Tower to Westminster; he did not visit the Tower again. The buildings of the medieval palace, around the White Tower, were now demolished and the bridge between St Thomas's and the Wakefield Towers was removed. In 1674 the bodies thought to be those of the two princes were found, in rubble below a staircase leading to the Chapel of St John. In place of the old palace, storehouses and offices were built for the Office of Ordnance, which was in charge of the arsenal at the Tower and of supplying the King's armouries and fleets. One of these buildings survives, the 'New Armouries'. The remainder seem to have been along the inner northern wall between the Martin and Devereux Towers plus storage on the Wharf and in the White Tower. The Tower was properly secured and garrisoned, the Moat was cleaned to make the living areas more habitable; a retaining wall was built round the outer edge of the Moat and the Iron Gate was demolished, leaving the Tower totally surrounded by water. Platforms were built on the ramparts to take some ninety guns and the corner bastions—Legge's Mount and Brass Mount—were rebuilt as gun emplacements. Charles regarded the Tower as a useful refuge if there were any challenge to his power.

It was not until after the Restoration, in 1661, that the Armouries became a museum open to the general public. The famous 'Line of Kings' dates from this period; its wooden horses and figures, displaying historic armour, were made by famous wood-carvers such as Grinling Gibbons and John Nost (whose horses can be seen in the Royal Armouries today). The figures represented most of the Kings of England from William the Conqueror to Charles II, but only Henry VIII and Charles I wore their own armour. During the eighteenth century further figures were added up to George II but it was never a complete record of monarchs. The 'Line' was a magnificent spectacle but a disaster in terms of historical accuracy and it was not until the nineteenth century that attempts were made to correct the errors. It was housed in the Horse Armoury (1664) (now the New Armouries).

The Spanish Armoury commemorated the defeat of the Armada (1588) and contained

*Sally Port and the Byward Tower seen from the Wharf. Royal and distinguished visitors arriving by river landed at the Queen's Stairs and entered by a postern in the Byward Tower.*

relics of that battle and instruments of torture, mostly of doubtful authenticity. Nevertheless, it was very popular and was located in Coldharbour, south-west of the White Tower. The Grand Storehouse, started in 1688, contained historic and captured trophies as well as vast quantities of modern small arms and cannons.

Since the fourteenth century, London had been the political and administrative capital of England, with Westminster as the permanent home of the offices of government and justice, but it was also the national market-place. It was full of narrow streets, timber-framed and plaster houses, a multiplicity of small shops, craftsmen's workshops, and markets which handled commodities for home and overseas. There was a large immigrant population and it was desperately crowded, vulnerable to both pestilence and fire.

The great plague (1665) caused a number of Tower inhabitants to be removed to the pest house in Stepney, where they mostly recovered. The Tower escaped the Great Fire of London (1666) through a fortunate change of wind; since the buildings were full of gunpowder at the time, a fire would have resulted in cataclysmic damage. These major disruptions apart, the Tower was a hive of industry. It was still a substantial prison, the Mint was thriving and in 1662 new coinage methods were instituted (la Belle Stuart was the model for Britannia), the Ordnance Office was working to full capacity, and the Royal Armouries were functioning as a major museum. The Menagerie was a popular attraction and the Crown Jewels could be seen on public display for the first time.

After Charles I's death Parliament had dispersed the Crown Jewels and Plate by sale, or by melting them down for coinage. Sir Thomas Viner was given the task of producing a new set of Regalia for the coronation of Charles II, his nephew, Sir Robert Viner, becoming the Crown Jeweller. It is this Regalia that forms the core of the collection on display at the Tower today. The Crown Jewels were moved to the Martin Tower in 1669 and put in the charge of Talbot Edwards; he became the first Keeper of the

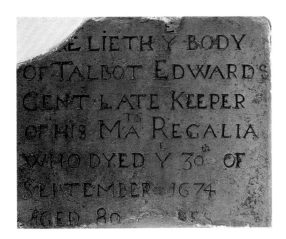

The gravestone of Talbot Edwards, the first 'Keeper of the Regalia at the Tower of London', who died in 1674. The stone was found just outside the Beauchamp Tower and is now set in the south wall of the Chapel of St Peter ad Vincula.

Regalia at the Tower of London. The Master and Treasurer of the Jewels and Plate was Sir Gilbert Talbot who had no intention of living in the Tower. He failed to persuade the King to pay a salary to Talbot Edwards, but did secure permission for the Keeper to allow members of the public to see the Jewels on payment of an entrance fee; this proved a great financial success for Edwards.

In 1671 Thomas Blood ('Colonel Blood') made his famous attempt to steal the Crown Jewels. He was an Irish renegade of several aliases, who posed as a clergyman and ingratiated himself with the Edwards family; they lived in the upper half of the Martin Tower, the Crown Jewels being kept in the basement in a locked cupboard. Blood went so far as to suggest that his nephew, a supposedly rich man, might make a match for the Edwards's daughter. Blood arranged a meeting early one morning, and was accompanied by three of his friends. While waiting for Mrs Edwards to arrive he suggested a visit to the Crown Jewels. Once in the basement, they bound and gagged Edwards, hit him on the head with a mallet because he made too much noise, and threatened him with a dagger. The villains were unexpectedly interrupted by Edwards's son, an army officer, returning home on leave from Flanders. Blood stabbed the old man and, with his fellow conspirators, rushed off with the Crown, the Sceptre, and the Orb. Blood and one accomplice, Parrot, were cap-

tured near the present East Gate, the Crown by then rolling in the gutter. The other two reached their horses at the Iron Gate and escaped. Blood was put in the White Tower, but was in no way abashed by the episode, and was later pardoned and given a pension by Charles II. Rumours abounded that it was a put-up job, as Charles was short of money, but it seems more likely that Blood knew too much about the murky past of Buckingham, the King's friend, to be put on open trial where he could have been a major embarrassment; in addition, Blood was well placed to be a very good spy against the Irish. Talbot Edwards recovered and died in 1674, at the age of eighty. His gravestone, found by the Beauchamp Tower, is set in the south wall of the Chapel of St Peter ad Vincula.

Charles was a keen astronomer and astrologer. He appointed Sir John Flamstead Astronomer Royal and in 1675 the Royal Observatory was created in the north-east turret of the White Tower. From this stems the story of the Ravens of the Tower. To the east of the Tower was a built-up area and then open country and ravens were common birds. They are scavengers and meat-eaters; it was an excellent feeding area for them and they multiplied. Charles was looking through his telescopes one day, with Sir John Flamstead by his side, when some ravens flew overhead and bespattered the telescopes. Charles was furious. 'These ravens must go!' he said. 'But, Sire, it is very unlucky to kill a raven', replied Flamstead, 'if you do that the Tower will fall and you will lose your kingdom, having only just got it back!' Charles, being a pragmatist, thought for a moment and said: 'The Observatory must go to Greenwich and the ravens can stay in the Tower.' Of all the reasons for the Royal Observatory being moved to Greenwich this must be the most attractive, although I cannot vouch for its accuracy.

In 1668, the well known Quaker William Penn was sent to the Tower for publishing a violent attack on established religious beliefs in a pamphlet 'The Sandy Foundation Shaken'. He was imprisoned in the attics of the Queen's House, south-west corner gable, where he wrote

*View from the Council Chamber
of the Queen's House.*

his book *No Cross, No Crown*. On arrival he stated: 'The Tower is to me the worst possible argument in the world. My prison shall be my grave before I will budge a jot.' Penn lived to found Pennsylvania in 1681, then known as Sylvania. It is said that Charles added the 'Penn' when signing the deed granting Penn proprietary rights in the territory: an apocryphal story which could be true.

Samuel Pepys flits through the period. He escorted Charles back to England at the Restoration and was a constant visitor to the Tower. Much to his surprise he became a prisoner there for a few weeks in 1679, and it took a year before all charges against him were finally dropped. This stemmed from the infamous Titus Oates revelations which implicated most well-known Catholics in a plot to hasten the succession of James. Many were sent to the Tower but only Viscount Stafford was executed. The anti-Catholic revulsion, whipped up by the Oates revelations, caused Charles to advise his brother James, the heir to the throne, to leave the country. James agreed, establishing himself in Scotland, but asked that Monmouth (Charles's eldest bastard son) should leave as well; he did not want the field left open for a Protestant take-over should Charles, already in bad health, die suddenly. This was agreed by Monmouth who withdrew to Holland but returned after two months, to the fury of the King, who stripped him of his titles. Monmouth played Judas to his Protestant supporters, blaming them for everything; Lord Russell, Algernon Sidney, and the Earl of Essex went to the block. Charles II died just over a year later, in February 1685, and was succeeded by his brother James II (1685–89).

Three months later the Duke of Monmouth landed at Lyme Regis proclaiming himself King Monmouth. The battle of Sedgemoor ended his dream and, despite abject pleadings with the King, he was executed on 15 July 1685 at Tower Hill; the executioner was the notorious Jack Ketch, who, according to the story told by many Yeoman Warders, took five strokes of the axe to sever the head which he then held high for all to

see. 'Behold, the head of a traitor!' It was only then that it was realised that no portrait existed of the Duke. The head was sewn back on the body so that a portrait could be painted before the burial in St Peter ad Vincula (the body lies under the altar). This, the Yeoman Warders say, is why the portrait in the National Portrait Gallery has such a pale face.

On 11 June 1685 the troops in the Tower were formed into the Royal Regiment of Fusiliers under George Legge, Lord Dartmouth, who was Master General of the Ordnance. In 1689 Legge was dismissed and imprisoned in the Tower, either for his Catholic connections or for being a supporter of the exiled James, and the Regiment was sent overseas. It did not renew its association with the Tower until 1949 when, after 260 years, the City of London Headquarters, the Home Headquarters of the Royal Regiment of Fusiliers, and the Regimental Museum, were located there once again.

Against all advice, James proceeded to bring Catholics back into positions of power and persecuted anyone remotely connected with the Monmouth rebellion. The 'Bloody Assizes' under Judge Jeffreys, who became James's Lord Chancellor, were notorious for such persecutions. James's campaign culminated when the Archbishop of Canterbury and six other bishops were committed for trial at the Tower for protesting at the Edict of Toleration, issued by James. They were found not guilty, James's position became untenable, and as a result William and Mary were invited, by a group of peers, to take the throne. James, with the Queen and Prince of Wales withdrew to France, spitefully throwing the Great Seal into the Thames, but taking with him some of the Crown Jewels including the Stuart Sapphire, now at the back of the Imperial State Crown.

William III (1689–1702) and Mary II (1689–94) were King and Queen each in their own right: William refused to be Consort to his wife who, indeed, agreed with his chauvinist views. Mary was the eldest daughter of James II by his first wife the Protestant Anne Hyde, while William was the son of James's sister, yet another

Mary; thus they were first cousins and both had clear links to the throne. An additional set of Regalia was therefore needed, which is why there are two Orbs in the Crown collection (Mary's Orb was used for the coronations of Queen Anne, George I, George II, and George III, but George IV characteristically insisted on the larger Charles II Orb). Both Orbs were placed on the coffin of Queen Victoria at her funeral.) Lord Lucas became Constable of the Tower and in 1691 the King and Queen gave him the Altar Dish and Flagon which are today displayed on the altar of the Chapel of St Peter ad Vincula at Christmas, Easter and Whitsun; the rest of the year they are on public view with the remainder of the Plate and Regalia.

Judge Jeffreys met his end in the Tower in 1689, dying of a surfeit of alcohol. He was allowed unlimited brandy, for he was a sick man close to death and in pain. He had stayed as Chancellor to the end, but when James abdicated he tried to escape retribution by hiding in a ship at Wapping. He was recognised and ended his days in the Bloody Tower. £37,000 was found with him—no small sum for those days. No one wanted his body so it was buried in St Peter ad Vincula, though later it was removed by his family and buried elsewhere.

In 1686 the question of the Tower Liberties (boundaries) was resolved, always a sore point between the City, the Hamlets around the Tower, and the Tower authorities. Stones and visible marks were positioned and jurisdictions defined. Thus is explained the challenge by the Chaplain in the ceremony of the Beating of the Bounds: 'Cursed is he that removeth his neighbours' landmark.' By 1692 the Grand Storehouse was finished (replaced by the Waterloo Block in 1845) and a grand banquet was given for William and Mary. Sir Christopher Wren was commissioned to renovate the Bloody and Beauchamp Towers as prison lodgings; he also changed the character of the Martin Tower by modernising and rebuilding.

The Tower was still full of prisoners but its nature as a prison had changed, now being used, primarily, for State prisoners entitled to a fair degree of comfort. No longer was it full of prisoners of war or unfortunates destined to be put under dire restraint, even torture. Prisoners paid for their accommodation and food; they were often accompanied by servants and allowed the freedom of the Tower during daylight hours. Only three Tower prisoners were executed for treason—John Ashton at Tyburn in 1691, Sir William Parkyns and Sir John Fenwick who had plotted King William's assassination in 1696.

The Mint was busy and in the 1690s brought in a complete new set of silver coinage. In 1699 the great Sir Isaac Newton was appointed Master of the Mint; by now the old problem of rogues clipping the coinage had been made impractical.

Mary II died of smallpox in 1694 leaving William to reign alone until his death in 1702, when Queen Anne (1702–14) succeeded. She had little to do with the Tower and it was not until the early years of the reign of George I, that it returned to prominence, or notoriety, through the executions resulting from the Jacobite rebellions.

# V

# *The Hanoverians*

# 1714–1837

During the eighteenth century the Tower disappeared from the national stage and changed in character. It was no longer a major prison, although still used in times of emergency or special circumstances. Hanging replaced the more gory methods of execution, the last execution by axe on Tower Hill was that of Lord Lovat in 1747. A mix of soldiers, workmen, craftsmen, and office workers supported the activities of the Army, the Mint, the Board of Ordnance and the Public Record Office.

In addition, the Tower was being developed as a major attraction for visitors. The tour started at the Menagerie, where an admission offering, sometimes accepted, was a live dog or cat to be fed to the animals. By 1741 the animals had been listed, all were named, and there was an entrance fee of 6d rising to 1s by the end of the century; this was a substantial sum. There was a high mortality rate and it is likely that the conditions for the animals were not good and probably extremely cramped. From here visitors went to the Middle Tower where they would be met by a Yeoman Warder guide, in the same area as the start of the present-day Yeoman Warders' tours. They were escorted to see the varying displays of the Armouries, such as the Spanish Armoury, the Grand Storehouse, and the 'Line of Kings'. For the bawdy, there was the figure of Henry VIII wearing the codpiece from the Greenwich Armour; the codpiece could be activated mechanically by pressing a switch.

*The River Thames from St Thomas's Tower.*

The last part of the visitors' tour was a visit to the Jewel House in the Martin Tower where the Crown Jewels were kept behind bars, rather than in the locked cabinet of Talbot Edwards's day. The display was hopelessly conceived and no attempt was made to explain the history of the exhibits. Visitors were allowed to reach through the bars and handle the Regalia. This practice was halted in 1815 after a mad woman wrenched apart the arches on the State Crown, which cost ten guineas to repair.

After the Grand Storehouse was completed in 1692 there was no major building in the Tower until the reconstruction of the Ordnance Storehouses, a century later. Building of housing continued (the residents numbered more than 1,000), although many of these dwellings no longer exist; the area now known as the Casemates (meaning 'houses within the walls') was developed and many Yeoman Warders live there today. Rather more significant was the widening of some windows in the White Tower and the drastic renovation of the Middle Tower.

My own home, St Thomas's Tower, was used as an infirmary and a pumping station; in 1743 one soldier committed suicide by jumping into the Moat while in a crazed condition. I have the architects' drawings which include the water engine that was installed in 1721, and it was from these drawings that I was able to explain a ghostly incident that took place some five years ago. I awoke from a deep sleep to see a door open

*The Casemates (houses within the walls), first built in the eighteenth century and completed during the nineteenth. This one is now the home of Yeoman Warder Kenny.*

in the wall close to my bed (there is no door there); it closed slowly as though someone had seen my wife and myself, but did not want to disturb us. The old plan showed the door at the exact position in the wall where my ghostly visitor had looked at the present tenants.

Although the Tower had become relatively humdrum there were periods when it reverted to its former notoriety. One of these was the First Jacobite Rebellion of 1715. The first Hanoverian King George I (1714–27) was a distant cousin of Queen Anne. (His claim to the throne came through Elizabeth of Bohemia the daughter of James I, and her daughter Sophia the Electress of Hanover, who was George's mother.) He spoke fluent French, but little English, and was better known as a fighter than a man of intellect. Like many Germans he had an ear for music and it is said that Handel, to appease the King when he was in disfavour, hired a barge to follow him from Whitechapel to Limehouse; a small orchestra played the new piece now known as Handel's 'Water Music'. There was trouble from the Old Pretender, James Edward Stuart, the son of James II, who landed in Scotland, but gained insufficient support seriously to threaten the King. Some example had to be made however, and three Scottish peers were sent to the block. Earl Derwentwater and Viscount Kenmure were executed on 24 February 1716, but the third, William Maxwell, Earl of Nithsdale, escaped on the eve of his execution; it was the most romantic and dramatic escape of the Tower's history.

Lady Nithsdale, the young, good-looking wife of the Earl, was determined to save her husband from the scaffold. She rode to London from Scotland, as the weather was too bad for the stagecoaches, and asked for an audience with the King. He refused to see her, but she waylaid him coming from a reception, and threw herself on the floor clutching his cloak, pleading for clemency for her husband. She was dragged away by officials and realised that the only solution was to plan her husband's escape from the Tower on the eve of his execution. She plotted with her landlady, Mrs Mills, involved her maid, Evans, and brought in Miss Hilton, a friend of Mrs Mills. Lord Nithsdale was held in the Lieutenant's Lodgings (the present Queen's House) in a room next to, and connected with, the Council Chamber which was used as a guardroom for the five Yeoman Warders assigned to watch over him. Lady Nithsdale gained the goodwill and sympathy of these Yeoman Warders by a mixture of bribery and charm as, in any event, they had no personal animosity towards the prisoner. She had first to persuade her husband to agree to her plan of escape which involved disguising him as a woman. He was a proud man and could face execution but not the ridicule that he would suffer if recaptured in female clothes. The plan was complex and involved creating a lot of confusion which would allow Nithsdale to escape, posing as one of his wife's friends. Mrs Mills was a big woman and Miss Hilton was tall and thin so both could wear additional clothing—Miss Hilton an extra cloak, and Mrs Mills an additional dress. The party arrived at Queen's House and Evans, the maid, was posted on the staircase so that her mistress could shout messages to her. There was much weeping and the Warders were upset at seeing such distress. First Miss Hilton was taken in to Lord Nithsdale, depositing her extra cloak, then Mrs Mills, leaving her extra dress but putting on the Hilton cloak. She was led out by Lady Nithsdale, who created confusion by shouting instructions to her maid and generally caused the Warders to overlook Miss Hilton's exit. Mrs Mills left as Miss Hilton—complicated, but effective. Lord Nithsdale was then sent out, dressed as Mrs Mills, Lady Nithsdale remaining in his room to carry on a conversation with herself as though she were still talking to her husband. The Warders were also put off guard as she had told them that her husband was being pardoned and that her worry was that the pardon would not be collected in time that night. Lady Nithsdale then left, dropping the latch on the door and saying that unless the pardon arrived her husband was going to fast unto death and was not to be disturbed. This was just in time as supper was, even then, coming up the stairs. Her husband escaped to the Continent

two days later, disguised as a servant on the Venetian Ambassador's boat. Lady Nithsdale rode back to Scotland to secure the deeds of their lands, which would otherwise have been forfeited to the King, before joining her husband on the Continent. The Nithsdales lived happily in Rome for the rest of their lives.

George II (1727–60) was a good soldier and, in his younger days, did well at Oudenarde under Marlborough; at the age of sixty he was the last British sovereign to take part in a battle when he led his troops at Dettingen. He was proud to be English but retained his German accent and, like his father before him, was always at odds with his eldest son. In one angry moment he refused to let Prince Frederick Louis use the royal christening font for the baptism of his eldest child (later George III); he had to make do with a less ornate silver-gilt basin (now on display in the Jewel House with the Lily Christening Font).

In 1745 the Second Jacobite Rebellion was started by Charles Edward Stuart, the Young Pretender, making his attempt to recover the Crown. He had considerable initial success, getting as far south as Derby, but the battle of Culloden in April 1746 put paid to his hopes, and the Scottish troops were routed. Once again the Tower held prisoners for execution, and on 18 August 1746 the axe fell on the necks of the Earl of Kilmarnock and Lord Balmerino. Nine months later the eighty-year-old Simon Fraser, Lord Lovat, followed and had the doubtful distinction of being the last man to be beheaded on Tower Hill (the block and axe used for his execution are still on display in the Bowyer Tower). He was a disgraceful old man who had been involved in rape, pillage and murder but he rather enjoyed his execution, exchanging insults with all and sundry en route. He needed assistance to mount the scaffold and his last words were 'God save us, why should there be such a bustle about taking off an old grey head that cannot go up three steps without three bodies to support it.' He made a good end in front of an appreciative audience, the unprecedented numbers causing a stand to collapse, killing some twenty spectators. After 125 beheadings, Tower

*The Council Chamber, showing the plaque commemorating the discovery of the Gunpowder Plot. Guy Fawkes was interrogated here.*

Hill was last used as a place of execution in 1780 for three hangings.

George III (1760–1820) was more renowned for his loss of the American colonies than for his activities in England. He had two short periods of madness, in 1765 and 1788, and finally lost his sanity in 1811, the Prince of Wales (later George IV) acting as Regent. One American did find himself a prisoner in the Tower during this period, Henry Laurens, the Vice-President of South Carolina whose ship was intercepted en route to Holland in August 1780. As a declared rebel he ended in the Tower where he spent the next year, until exchanged for Lord Cornwallis, who had surrendered at Yorktown. 'Tower' Laurens became his nickname when he returned to America and he wrote a none too complimentary book about his confinement.

The war against Napoleon placed great pressure on the Tower and was a major factor in the decision to move the Mint, whose need for new steam engines was used as an opportunity to relocate staff and workshops in the Minories, just outside the Tower, this being completed by August 1812, the space now available being quickly occupied by the Army. Meanwhile, Ordnance buildings expanded on to Tower Wharf and were used for the provision of arms for continental battles, the overriding priority.

After the end of the war in 1815, some retrenchment took place and the Tower turned more towards attracting visitors again. The displays of the Armouries were re-housed and better presented and the Menagerie was put under new management. George IV (1820–30) at last succeeded his mad father, and in 1826 he appointed the Duke of Wellington Constable of the Tower. Wellington decided to concentrate on making the Tower a much more suitable barracks for housing soldiers and, during his tenure until his death in 1852, he continued to be preoccupied with the Tower's military role. During the 1840s increased pressure from Parliament and from Prince Albert, forced him to consider the Tower as a national monument that would attract tourists and provide an income for its upkeep.

By 1815 the Menagerie was in a sad state but

*The axe and block used for the last execution by this method, that of Simon Fraser, the eighty-year-old Lord Lovat condemned for his part in the second Jacobite rebellion in 1745.*

there was a dramatic improvement when, in 1822, a new Keeper was appointed, Alfred Cops. He improved the cages, reorganised the Menagerie and constructed an aviary and a small animal house. However, he was too successful and the number of animals kept, and the staff needed to maintain them, were too much for the limited space available in the Tower. Noise and hygiene were additional problems. Wellington therefore persuaded George's successor, William IV (1830–37), to move the collection to Regent's Park where a new zoo had been started in 1826. There was much opposition but Wellington prevailed, and by 1834 the animals were gone, the cages and buildings being dismantled by 1835.

One of Wellington's first acts was to reorganise the Yeoman Warders into a Body, with terms of service more similar to those of today. The buying and selling of posts was forbidden; the Yeoman Body became a regular paid service, and its members were recruited from ex-Army non-commissioned officers, not below the rank of Sergeant. All this was completed in 1827 and the 'Beefeaters' were given an additional allowance to replace their daily rations. An old record of the rations given to the Yeoman of the Guard dated 1813 gives some indication of where the term 'Beefeater' originated (the Yeoman Warders were on similar scales). Thirty men were given a daily ration of 37 gallons of beer, 24 lb of beef, 18 lb of mutton, and 16 lb of veal plus quantities of bread and vegetables.

The greatest impact made on the Tower by George IV was perhaps in refurbishing the Crown Jewels. He was determined to have the biggest and best coronation ever and the Crown Jewellers—Rundell, Bridge & Rundell—were instructed to update the Regalia, bring out all the Plate, and in addition make a new personal sword for the sovereign. This was the Jewelled State Sword (on display in the Jewel House) which cost £5,998 in 1821 and is worth several million pounds today. George's coronation robes (also on display in the Jewel House) were made of gold thread. His was the last official coronation banquet; the old-style banquet followed on

*Yeoman Warder David in 'Blue Undress', the uniform introduced in the Victorian period and now worn for normal duties.*

*The Jewelled State Sword made for the coronation of George IV in 1821.*

from the coronation, rather like a wedding breakfast, whereas the present custom is for a dinner to be held at Buckingham Palace.

Unlike his predecessor George IV, William IV (1830–37) detested extravagance and his coronation was at minimum cost. In his reign it was decided to use the same coronation rings for subsequent sovereigns and consorts; previously they had been regarded as the sovereigns' personal possessions and were renewed for each coronation. Consequently the Coronation Ring (the 'wedding ring of England'), last used in 1953 for Elizabeth II, was made for William IV and the Queen Consort's Ring was made for Queen Adelaide.

The Tower moved into the Victorian era under the strong hand of Wellington who was to make many changes, most of which have survived to this day.

# VI
# Queen Victoria
## 1837–1901

Queen Victoria was a great writer and more is known of her from her journals and letters than from any contemporary account. She was truthful, adaptable to change but not to people, and possessed a character that was moulded by events over the long period of her reign. She chose her advisers well and this was particularly fortunate for the Tower, as it was served by some excellent administrators; Prince Albert was an added, and important, influence.

The Duke of Wellington, Constable from 1826 until his death in 1852, was the greatest innovator in the history of the Tower, certainly in post-Restoration times. He was determined to rid the Tower of its peripheral interests. The Mint had already departed, the Menagerie followed in 1834 and the Board of Ordnance went in 1845. Wellington started the move of the Public Record Office, which was split between the White Tower and the Wakefield Tower. (It was not until 1867, well after Wellington's death, that the Public Record Office finally departed, leaving the Wakefield Tower to become, in 1869, the repository for the Crown Jewels.)

On 30 October 1841 the Grand Storehouse was destroyed by a fire which began in the Bowyer Tower (probably an overheated flue) and spread via the Grand Storehouse to the Martin Tower, threatening the safety of the Crown Jewels. It was a chaotic situation. There was enough water for only one of the nine hand-

*The tomb made for Sir Richard Cholmondeley, Lieutenant of the Tower during the reign of Henry VIII. The tomb was never used but when opened during the refurbishing of the Chapel of St Peter ad Vincula in 1876 it was found to contain a fourteenth-century christening font saved from Cromwell's troops who destroyed them throughout the country.*

operated fire engines; the Major of the Tower (Resident Governor) called for assistance from the London Fire Engine Establishment, but his order to close the Tower to unwelcome spectators was taken so literally that firemen were denied entry by the soldiers. By the time this nonsense was rectified, the firemen were restricted to playing their hoses on to the Martin and White Towers, and the Chapel, to prevent the fire spreading further. The fire now began to threaten the Jewel House which was located in the basement of the Martin Tower. Although the Keeper of the Crown Jewels, Edmund Swifte, had access to the chamber in which the Crown Jewels were kept, the keys to the display cases were held by the Lord Chamberlain's Department. By 11.00 pm something had to be done and Swifte, accompanied by Superintendent Pierse and officers of 'H' Division of the City Police, attacked the showcases and prised the protective bars apart. Yeoman Warders carried the Crown Jewels to the Queen's House, where they remained for a week, before being sent to Rundell, Bridge & Rundell, the Crown Jewellers, for cleaning and repair. They remained there until the new Jewel House by the side of the Martin Tower, providentially already under construction, was opened on 26 March 1842.

Swifte's income from visitors in 1838 and 1839 made the Treasury realise that they should take over this gold-mine and put the Keeper and his assistants on a fixed salary. A new Jewel

House was needed, to maximise income, and in 1840 work was started on a site just to the south of the Martin Tower. Consequently, the fire of 1841 did not prevent the Jewels being displayed to the public for more than five months, which was fortuitous indeed. In the event, the new Jewel House proved a failure, being damp and gloomy, but it was not until 23 April 1869 that the Crown Jewels were moved to the Wakefield Tower. In 1852 Queen Victoria herself had a hand in the appointment of the new Keeper of the Jewel House, Lieutenant Colonel Charles Wyndham, formerly of the Royal Scots Greys, and it was he who pressed for the move of the Crown Jewels to the Wakefield Tower and also for his own residence to be in St Thomas's Tower rather than in the Martin Tower. Salvin designed the Jewel Chamber and also the arch linking St Thomas's with the Wakefield, the old arch having been removed in the days of Charles II.

In 1855 the bracelet which had held the Koh-i-Noor Diamond went on display in the Jewel House. This bracelet was meant to be worn on the upper arm and there are pictures of Ranjit Singh, the Lion of the Punjab, wearing it in that manner. The three diamonds in it were replaced by crystals and the Koh-i-Noor is now in Queen Elizabeth the Queen Mother's Crown; the other two diamonds are in the Queen's personal jewellery.

The legend of the Koh-i-Noor goes back some 3,000 years and is wrapped in mythology. The present diamond is not that old although it is the oldest known major diamond in the world. There has always been confusion over its history as three major diamonds—Babur's diamond, the Great Mogul and the Koh-i-Noor—could be the same diamond called by three different names. It is likely that the diamond on display today was found in the Kollur mine in the Golkonda region of India in 1655, and weighed some 787 carats. It was presented by its owner, Mir Jumla, to Shah Jahan (who built the Taj Mahal) and was disgracefully cut down to 280 carats by a Venetian cutter, Hortensio Borgio, who was fined for his pains. In 1739 Delhi was sacked by Nadir Shah (ruler of Persia) and, as he did not have the

*Four world-famous precious stones: the First Star of Africa, 530 carats; the Second Star of Africa, 317 carats; the Koh-i-Noor diamond, 106 carats; the Stuart Sapphire, 104 carats.*

manpower to maintain his sovereignty, he gave Delhi back to its original owner, Mohammed Shah. Nadir Shah knew of a big diamond owned by the Delhi ruler who concealed it in his turban (intelligence gained through the harem). Consequently, he arranged a banquet at which he insisted on exchanging turbans with Mohammed Shah (a sign of amity that could not be refused). He rushed off to his tent, unwrapped the turban, and found the big diamond, exclaiming 'Koh-i-Noor' (Persian for 'Mountain of Light'). This is the Jewel House story of how the diamond was given its modern name.

The diamond then went on its travels. From India it went to Persia (1739), thence to Afghanistan (1751), and back to India (1813) where it came into the hands of Ranjit Singh. In 1849, on the annexation of the Punjab, it was claimed by the British and presented to Queen Victoria and put on display at the Great Exhibition in 1851. Prince Albert, among many others, was disappointed in the diamond's lack of fire and it was decided to have it re-cut to a more modern style. By this time it weighed 186 carats and Garrard, the Crown Jeweller, entrusted the cutting to a Dutch craftsman, Voorsanger, who ended with a modified brilliant of 106 carats. Most men who owned the stone suffered severe misfortune so it is placed in the Queen Consort's Crown as it is considered unlucky for any man to be its owner. The Koh-i-Noor has a dreadful history of murder—brothers blinding brothers—and one man who tried to possess it, Agha Mohammed, blinded 20,000 people after one of his battles and had the unpleasant habit of personally disembowelling any servant who displeased him!

In 1845 the Grand Storehouse was replaced by Waterloo Barracks. This was the beginning of the end of the Board of Ordnance in the Tower; its functions were taken over by the War Office some ten years later. Close by, and to the east of the new barracks, an Officers' Mess was built in the same style, now the headquarters of the Royal Regiment of Fusiliers and also their museum.

The year 1843 was an important one as, apart

*The Moat today, seen from the west with Beauchamp Tower behind. The grass represents water 20 feet deep, a formidable obstacle.*

from starting to build Waterloo Barracks, Wellington had the Moat drained and filled in as it was a nauseating health hazard. Massive Victorian sewers were constructed, and the Moat filled with 18 feet to 20 feet (5½ to 6 m) of earth and gravel; thus the level of the grass today represents a 20 feet (6 m) depth of water! When asked why the grass does so well and what is done to maintain this fine green vista, Yeoman Warders reply 'We cut it and roll it, cut it and roll it and, after 150 years, you get this result!'

Anthony Salvin (known for his work on Balliol College, Oxford) was an inspired choice as an architect, and it is his work that brought the Tower to its present-day state, so attractive to international, as well as British, tourists. The fire of 1841 entailed a lot of rebuilding, much of which was his work. He rebuilt the Bowyer Tower and restored both the Brick and the Martin Towers, all three having suffered from the fire. He demolished the Lion Barbican (1850) and then restored the upper part of the Salt Tower. Also in 1850 he started to bring the White Tower back to its former austere glory by removing the satellite building latched on to the west wall, although it was not until 1900 that the southern and eastern sides were cleared, leaving only the remains of the Wardrobe Tower on display. As an old man Salvin completed his work by rebuilding the Lanthorn Tower and re-establishing the curtain wall between the Wakefield, the Lanthorn, and the Salt Towers. The Ordnance Store that lay on the site of the old palace (the area of the present History Gallery) was demolished.

There was a period when military preparedness predominated—in the 1840s during the Chartist agitation. Wellington became nervous—revolution was in the air—and once again it became important to dominate Tower Hill and its area of the City. The North Bastion was constructed for this purpose but, in the event, the Chartists proved to have no substantial support. As supposed radical, dangerous rebels, their aims make interesting reading; they included annual parliaments, universal male suffrage (votes for women were considered, but

*The fifteenth-century tomb of the Duke of Exeter in the Chapel of St Peter ad Vincula.*

regarded as absurd), equal electoral districts, and removal of property qualifications for Members of Parliament. Yesterday's radical is, indeed, today's conservative!

Violence did happen, in 1885, when an explosion occurred in the White Tower which caused considerable damage but no serious injury; the fire-fighting lessons of 1841 had been learnt and the new fire service operated admirably. The bomb was planted by a Fenian fringe movement in support of Irish Home Rule; the culprit was caught and later sentenced to fourteen years' imprisonment.

It was Prince Albert, the Prince Consort, who was responsible for restoring the Chapel of St John in the White Tower after three hundred years of neglect. It had been used as a general storehouse, and repository for records, and was in an unimaginable state. The last Deputy Lieutenant, Lord de Ros, did a magnificent job in clearing out and bringing the Chapel back to its former Romanesque glory; it is today one of the more spectacular sights of the Tower.

In 1876 the first Resident Governor of the Tower, Colonel Sir Bryan Millman, presided over one of the major renovations of the period, that of the Chapel of St Peter ad Vincula. Salvin was consulted and the chapel was restored to its original Henry VIII style; its splendid Spanish chestnut ceiling was uncovered (it had been plastered over) and the west door was re-opened.

The stone flooring had to be taken up and replaced and, beneath the stones, were found the bones of hundreds of people (the estimate was 1,500 bodies). The sheer number was puzzling but it is quite possible that when the old parish church was moved to its present site the new location was the old graveyard. Furthermore, there were many burials in the chapel itself, particularly in the seventeenth and eighteenth centuries, when scant attention was paid to the bones of earlier corpses.

The graves of the more illustrious execution victims were known but there had been much desecration and not all could be identified. 'Two Dukes between two Queens' is quoted in many of the old histories and refers to Queen Anne

*The interior of the Chapel of St Peter ad Vincula, restored in the 1870s to its former Tudor Splendour.*

*The Chapel of St Peter ad Vincula.*

Boleyn, the Duke of Somerset (executed by Edward VI), the Duke of Northumberland (executed by Mary I, and father-in-law to Lady Jane Grey) and Queen Catherine Howard. The identification was a macabre task and the investigating Board did its best: the Duke of Monmouth lies under the altar, Anne Boleyn, Catherine Howard and Jane, Viscountess Rochford, are immediately in front. The second row includes the Duke of Somerset, General Sir John Fox Burgoyne, the Duke of Northumberland and Margaret, Countess of Salisbury. The other victims could not be identified among the mix-up of bones that were uncovered and were buried in the walls of the crypt in as respectful a manner as possible.

The sepulchre, now in the centre of the chapel, has moved full circle. It went from the centre to the north-west corner, then in 1876 to the east wall near the organ and finally in 1970 back to the centre. It was built between 1513 and 1519 (at the time of the chapel itself) by the Lieutenant of the Tower Sir Richard Cholmondeley, who was something of an autocrat. When the City was swept by riots in 1519, he fired off the Tower guns—an act not very popular with local residents. The story goes that it was not popular either with Henry VIII who lost his temper, banished Cholmondeley to the country and, out of spite, refused him permission to take his tomb with him. It was opened during the 1876 renovations and was found to contain a

*The memorial in the Chapel of St Peter ad Vincula to the family of George Payler, a seventeenth-century Master of the Ordinance.*

christening font (*c.* 1350), in four pieces, which is now located just inside the west entrance and is one of the three oldest christening fonts that exist of this pattern.

The area outside the Tower was changing rapidly to compete with the demands of the new docks and in 1827 the famous old Royal Hospital of St Katharine by the Tower was demolished. The Duke of Exeter's tomb (sometimes known as the 'Holland tomb'), originally housed there in a chantry chapel, went to the Foundation of St Katharine's chapel in Regent's Park where it stayed until the Foundation moved in 1950 to Radcliffe in East London. Queen Mary, the Patron of the Foundation, then asked that the tomb be moved to its present location in St Peter ad Vincula, as the Duke of Exeter had been a Constable of the Tower.

The Blount memorial (to the north of the altar) was dedicated to two Lieutenants of the Tower, father and son, Sir Richard Blount (1558–64) and Sir Michael Blount (1590). It was cleverly renovated in 1876. Opposite lies the monument to the family of George Payler, a seventeenth-century Master of the Ordnance.

The organ came to the Tower in 1890. It is one of the three oldest in England and was built by the renowned Father Bernhardt Schmidt in

*The final resting place of Anne*
*Boleyn and Catherine Howard in*
*the Chapel of St Peter ad Vincula.*

1699, the wood carving being by Grinling Gibbons. Its original home was in the Royal Chapel, Whitehall where it was rebuilt by Elliott in 1814 and further restored in 1953 by Wm Hill & Son and Norman & Beard Ltd. (The organ is in current use and can be heard by any member of the public who attends the regular Sunday services.)

The Thomas More memorial is a recent addition in the crypt and was placed there in 1970 but perhaps mention should be made of the silver Coptic Cross on the altar as, although the Cross is of this century, the wood comes from an old beam taken from the White Tower. The silver originated from the Queen of Sheba's mine in Abyssinia and the Cross was presented to the Royal Fusiliers by Emperor Haile Selassie, in gratitude for the Regiment's part in the Abyssinian campaign of the second world war.

Outside the Chapel, little was done other than general tidying. The two 'boxed' tombs are thought to belong to Ordnance families long departed, and the black stone near the southwest corner marks the resting place of the three ringleaders of the 103 deserters from Lord Sempil's Regiment (later the Black Watch). On 18 July 1743, they were executed in the Tower, their names being Farquhar Shaw, Malcolm MacPherson, and Samuel MacPherson. It is thought that the suicide from St Thomas's Tower, John Campbell, was buried with them.

Between 1826 and 1883, the 'Line of Kings' was located in the New Horse Armoury, a

*Yeoman Warder Hendley in State Dress.*

Gothic building on the south side of the White Tower. It had been rearranged by Dr Samuel Meyrick and, whilst more accurate, was not so spectacular. The building was pulled down in 1883 and the contents dispersed into the galleries of the White Tower. The Spanish Armoury, also heavily criticised by Meyrick, had its name changed to Queen Elizabeth's Armoury in 1831 and was moved in 1837 to the crypt of the Chapel of St John where it stayed until it was dispersed in the latter part of the century. The destruction by fire of the Grand Storehouse in 1841 caused heavy loss but Robert Porrett persuaded the Board of Ordnance to purchase more historic pieces and, together with John Hewitt, he reorganised the collection. The entrance fee in 1840 was 6d and there were 95,231 visitors. A separate charge was made for the Regalia.

In 1864 a sentry was court-martialled for deserting his post by Queen's House; he was found in a state of collapse. His story was that he saw a white figure making towards Queen's House. He gave a formal challenge, received no response, so made a tentative lunge with his bayonet. To his horror the bayonet went straight through the figure, meeting no resistance. At the court martial he was acquitted, as two independent witnesses had seen the white figure from the windows of the Bloody Tower. The phantom figure has been seen by other sentries over the years and the post has an evil reputation. Who was the figure? Perhaps Anne Boleyn, or Catherine Howard, or . . . ?

# VII

# The Tower
# in the Twentieth Century

By the time that Queen Victoria died in 1901, the Tower had become a major tourist attraction, although not quite to the extent it is today. It was still manned by a substantial number of troops, but its 'raison d'être' was as a useful barracks rather than a defensive fortress. Ceremonial duties and the guarding of the Crown Jewels were the preoccupation of the battalion living in the Tower as by then there was no thought of revolutionary activity affecting the Crown. The Crown Jewels replaced the Armouries as the most popular attraction though of course the Armouries had far more extensive displays and occupied a large proportion of the Tower.

The first world war did not have too much impact as the Tower remained open to visitors until the latter part of the conflict, when the Zeppelin bombings caused it to close and some of the Crown Jewels, together with the more valuable pieces in the Armouries' collection, were evacuated. One bomb fell in the north Moat but there was no substantial damage. After a long gap (1820–1914), the Tower was again used as a prison and place of execution. The first victim was Carl Hans Lody, a German spy who was shot by a firing squad in the East Casemates miniature Rifle Range. In 1915 nine more German spies were shot, and finally Zender Hurwitz was shot on 11 April 1916, making a total of eleven in all. A more famous man, Sir Roger Casement, was held prisoner in St

*The Tower in modern setting.*

Thomas's Tower before his execution by hanging at Pentonville on 3 August 1916. He tried to form an Irish Brigade of the German Army and was captured after landing from a submarine at Tralee in Ireland.

Between the wars, the Tower was briefly used as a prison for traitors when, on 26 January 1933, Norman Baillie-Stewart, an officer in the Seaforth Highlanders, was charged with passing information to the Germans. He took exercise in the Moat under an armed guard and was the subject of the newspaper headline 'Who is the officer in the Tower?' He was sentenced to five years penal servitude and, when released in 1938, went to Germany where he was employed with William Joyce (better known as Lord Haw-Haw). They were both arrested after the end of the war; Joyce was hanged but Baillie-Stewart was sent back to prison for five years. He eventually retired to Ireland.

On 3 September 1939 the Tower Prisoner of War Collection Centre became fully operational and received its first prisoners two weeks later. The Tower was closed to the public and the Crown Jewels moved to a place of safety, the location of which has never been disclosed. Over the next three months crewmen from the German submarines U-27, U-42 and U-35 passed through the Centre; additionally, there were a number of Luftwaffe personnel and, in all, about 180 men were processed before the Centre was moved to Cockfosters. Rudolf Hess came to

the Tower on 17 May 1941 and left on 21 May for Mytchett Place, Surrey; he was held in a room at the northern end of Queen's House, on the first floor. The war was not to pass without an execution in the Tower and Sergeant Josef Jacobs, a German spy who parachuted into England, was despatched by firing squad in the East Casemates Rifle Range on 4 August 1941. He had a damaged ankle and was seated for the shooting; the chair is still preserved in the Tower but is not displayed. Jacobs was the last person to be executed in the Tower after nearly 900 years of bloodstained history.

The bombing raids made the Tower unsuitable for holding prisoners and consequently it went on to a 'care and maintenance' basis until the end of the war. The Moat was dug up for allotments, providing a good supply of vegetables for the families of the Yeoman Warders. Much damage was done but luckily the major historic buildings escaped a direct hit. The North Bastion (c. 1840) and an ugly Victorian barrack

*Tourists with Yeoman Warder*
*Sharp as their guide.*

block were destroyed; the destruction of this barrack block (known as the Main Guard) was a blessing because it brought about the restoration of the old Henry III wall (c. 1240) which blends so much better with the White Tower. The roof of St Thomas's Tower was ruined and much minor damage occurred elsewhere. One Yeoman Warder, one Welsh Guardsman, and three others were killed in the Tower by enemy action. Throughout the war, the Ceremony of the Keys (the ceremonial closing of the Tower each evening) continued despite bombing interruptions. On one occasion, the Chief Yeoman Warder was blown off his feet by a bomb blast and had to apologise for the delay in the Ceremony.

Once the war was over, the Tower swiftly returned to normal and soon became the major attraction that it is today with some 2½ million visitors a year, coming from all parts of the world. The Moat reverted to grass and the ravens returned—there had been a gap (despite the legend)—and the business of international tourism became the major function of the Tower which is, now, for practical purposes a 'palace and fortress' in name only. The military presence is limited to a ceremonial guard (tactical when the Tower is closed), a small ordnance store (the Brass Mount), and the Home Headquarters of the Royal Regiment of Fusiliers.

Sadly, on 17 July 1974, a bomb exploded in the basement of the White Tower, killing one visitor and injuring some forty others. Although no one acknowledged responsibility for it, it was, clearly, one of the heartless terrorist attacks that seem to be symptomatic of the past two decades. The damage done was considerable, but the fabric withstood the blast, and all that can be seen today is a brass plaque commemorating this tragic event.

The sheer number of visitors made it imperative to make changes within the Tower to improve the amenities and better display the Crown Jewels, and the Arms and Armour. In 1967 the Crown Jewels were moved from the Wakefield Tower to the new Jewel House in the Waterloo Block which had been specially constructed within the fabric of the Victorian building. The Royal Armouries' superlative display of oriental armour was also located in the Waterloo Block, and an Education Centre established in the upper floors of the same building. A large percentage of Tower visitors are children—many of whom form part of school parties for whom there is a free entry scheme over the winter months. The Education Centre runs a comprehensive programme which includes lectures, film shows and drama; also the opportunity to dress up in armour and handle replicas of the Crown Jewels.

In 1982 the Queen opened the first phase of the Wall Walk which enables visitors to walk on the battlements, passing through a number of historic towers. The entry is from the Wakefield Tower and the visitor passes through the chamber where Henry VI was murdered, on to the battlements, and thence to the Salt Tower—notorious for its religious prisoners. The Walk then leads to the Broad Arrow Tower, which has a display of how it might have looked as a knight's bedroom in 1381, then through the Constable Tower to the Martin Tower (where the Crown Jewels were held at the time of Colonel Blood's attempt to steal them). The Royal Armouries also opened a new gallery in 1982 commemorating the Board of Ordnance, which includes a fine display of pistols and muskets suitable for viewing by the specialist as well as the curious visitor. There are plans to open up additional attractions for the public over the course of the next decade in response to the tremendous tourist demand.

The ravens deserve their own place as they are a tremendous attraction and are intelligent birds who are great mimics. One of the Yeoman Warders has the post of Ravenmaster and is regarded as 'Senior Raven' by the other birds: he has to be careful during the mating season as the male ravens think that he is 'chatting up' their wives. The wings of the ravens are clipped, a painless procedure, and they try to breed, but they have yet to be successful, although eggs have been laid. Ravens are notoriously difficult to breed in captivity as their natural environ-

ment requires more privacy and greater space than can be given in the Tower. Replacement ravens come from a variety of sources but are normally birds that have been brought up in captivity from fledgelings who would otherwise have perished in the wild. They live up to twenty years, although there is an amazing record of James Crow who survived for forty-four years. When a raven dies he is buried in the Moat; the graveyard can be seen from the Middle Draw-

*Raven Charlie inspecting troops.*

*(Overleaf) The floodlit Tower seen from the river.*

bridge, in the area close to St Thomas's Tower. All ravens are mischievous but occasionally we get one who misbehaves badly and has to be posted elsewhere. In the Tower, the ravens are regarded as people, witness the case of Raven George whose Tower Order reads: 'On Saturday, 13 September 1986, Raven George, enlisted in 1975, was posted to the Welsh Mountain Zoo. Conduct unsatisfactory, services therefore no longer required.' Six ravens are on establishment

and two further ravens are allowed as guests. As I write, the two guest ravens are half-grown, having been reared by hand from the age of six weeks. Their food comes from Smithfield's meat market (ravens are flesh-eaters), although biscuits and household scraps vary their diet. They are hardy and appear to thrive in the Tower, having a splendid roosting cage to return to each night; this is known as the 'Ravens' Hilton'!

All ravens love water and they have a number of bird-baths which they use constantly. The legend goes that they were originally white birds and were the first released by Noah from the Ark, but instead of returning and reporting progress they gorged themselves on the dead animals. God was furious and, as a punishment, turned the ravens black and said that they would always be in need of water. The better known story of the Tower falling if the ravens leave has some basis in fact, as the ravens did multiply and

*The Tower's regular soldiers, the Brigade of Guards, on parade.*

their increasing numbers became a nuisance, causing many complaints which could have led to their being banished.

Every raven has his own characteristics and they differ enormously. Some are quite lovable, others are vicious, all are unpredictable. One raven, Hector, could talk but became furious if people did not say 'Good morning, Hector' as they passed. He had to be posted to the London Zoo as he committed the cardinal sin of pecking the Resident Governor. The Tower might not fall if the ravens went, but it would lose some of its character.

The Tower is proud of its traditional ceremonies. The Ceremony of the Keys is perhaps the best known, and is attended by seventy visitors each night (no charge is made, tickets being supplied on application to the Tower). It is a short ceremonial closing of the Tower Gates culminating in the Guard being paraded at the

top of the Broad Walk Steps, and the Supervising Yeoman Warder doffing his Tudor bonnet as the clock strikes 10.00 pm, saying 'God preserve Queen Elizabeth', the Guard replying 'Amen'.

Not so well known, but rewarding to watch, is the changing of the Guard which takes place daily on Tower Green. The same battalion supplies the Guard for Buckingham Palace and Windsor, but the Tower provides the best spectacle. Another military event of surprising frequency, as the ravens could testify, is the use of the Tower as a Saluting Station. The Honour-

*Major General A. P. W. MacLellan, the Resident Governor, with escorting Yeoman Warders at the Christmas 1987 State Parade.*

*Pomp and circumstance: a selection of ceremonial dress items.*

able Artillery Company provide four 25-pounder guns for the salute which, depending on the event commemorated, is of sixty-two or forty-one guns. The higher figure is calculated as twenty-one guns for the Tower, twenty-one guns for the City of London, and one gun for each of the twenty towers where a saluting gun used to be located.

Christmas, Easter and Whitsun see State Parades of Yeoman Warders in full ceremonial dress escorting the Resident Governor from Queen's House to the Chapel of St Peter ad

Vincula, and back again after the service. Every five years there is a massive parade to celebrate the Installation of the Constable in which the Constable's late regiment, the Yeoman Warders, and the Brigade of Guards, are all represented. The keys of the Tower are presented by the Lord Chamberlain to the Constable, who passes them on to the Resident Governor. Whenever the Queen visits the Tower she is offered the keys back but luckily she always refuses them—otherwise, the Resident Governor woud have to find somewhere else to live.

Every three years there is the Beating of the Bounds which defines the ancient area of the Tower's boundaries. It is colourful and involves local school children beating the markers with sticks, challenges being made by the City, and responses made by the Resident Governor, resplendent in Full Dress uniform. It creates a marvellous traffic jam but City home-goers are remarkably tolerant.

Two private ceremonies occur which are not attended by the public. One is the annual ceremony of the Lilies and Roses commemorating the murder of Henry VI in the Wakefield Tower on 21 May 1471. During a short service by the Oratory in the Wakefield Tower the Provost of Eton lays lilies and the Provost of King's College, Cambridge lays roses—Henry VI being their founder. A small parade of the Tower Officers, Yeoman Warder Supervisors, Jewel House Curators and the two Provosts processes to and from Queen's House to the Wakefield Tower. The other ceremony is the swearing-in of new Yeoman Warders, conducted by the Resident Governor in the presence of his two Deputies and the Yeoman Body. After the formal swearing-in, all concerned repair to the Yeoman Warders' Club where a toast is made to the new Warder 'May you never die a Yeoman Warder!' This relates to the time when Yeoman Warders' posts were bought and sold but, if a Warder died in office, his post reverted to the Constable of the Tower and could not be sold by his family.

Once the public leaves the Tower becomes a village community. Some fifty-four families live in the Tower, mostly those of Yeoman Warders;

they have their own club, run by themselves, which is, in effect, the village 'pub'. They organise numerous social events and it is a very 'go-ahead' concern. The bowls team is much in evidence during the summer months and guest teams are entranced at playing in the Moat, and even more entranced at the refreshments later provided in the Yeoman Warders' Club.

The Moat becomes the public park for residents who walk their dogs, play tennis and, sometimes, cricket; even football and rugby practices occur when enthusiasts, generally teenage sons and daughters of residents, have a mind to organise a session. Most of the residents have an ex-Service background so tend to have a number of interests in common, thus creating a friendly community atmosphere, very necessary in such an enclosed society. From time to time there is a Christmas pantomime which raises considerable sums for charity and also punctures the egos of many of the residents who are, good-humouredly, lampooned by the playwright (he normally goes on holiday immediately after the last performance!).

Entry and exit from the Tower can be a problem as cars cannot leave after the Ceremony of the Keys at 10 pm. Inhabitants on foot can use the wicket gate until midnight but after that special arrangements must be made for entry up to 3 am; exiting after midnight is not allowed. Between 3 am and 6.45 am entry and exit is only with the specific permission of the Resident Governor. Tower children are well used to the restrictions but some teenagers, forgetful about carrying their passes, have had awkward moments trying to persuade a Gurkha sentry that they live in the Tower. (The Brigade of Guards do not always provide the sentries.)

The uniform of the Yeoman Warders can cause problems as it is very difficult, if not impossible, to put on the State Dress without help. The wives become dressers and it is hilarious when there are bachelors in the Body who have to be helped by their friends' wives. Serious consideration is being given to producing Yeoman Warders' 'tights' as there are problems in obtaining suitable girdles to fit their figures

and hold their stockings up. These are difficulties that the general public do not appreciate. At Christmas, the Resident Governor holds a party for all Tower residents and the Warders reciprocate with an excellent buffet supper in the Yeoman Warders' Club. It is an unusually close community and a happy one; it is rare indeed for a Yeoman Warder to resign.

The task of repair and maintenance of the Tower's fabric is endless, which perhaps helps to explain a peculiarity of at least one of its ghosts. The St Thomas's Tower ghost does not care for workmen and often manifests himself after they have left, sometimes creating more problems. The back doorway to St Thomas's, under the arch leading to the Wakefield Tower, is no longer in use and is permanently locked. Inside, the original stone steps (c. 1280) lead up to the roof. There is no access to them other than through our living quarters. The arrow slits have glass windows on the inside, to keep the birds out, fixed quite firmly, in a similar fashion to the external windows of a normal house. We once had to move some furniture into the Oratory as a temporary measure, but perhaps we should have known better as our ghost does not care for any tampering with his Oratory. The following morning I had to check the roof and found that a window-frame had been removed from an arrow slit and carefully placed some ten stone steps lower. It could not have fallen out without being damaged, and our carpenter later confirmed that the removal looked like a professional job. No human being could possibly have been there, so perhaps the ghost was making a point. But it is a mystery we cannot solve.

Yeoman Warder David at ease
with friends.

Yeoman Warder Pritchard's front
door.

St Thomas's Tower, home of the author and resident ghost.

(Overleaf) The Tower of London today, covering an area of 18 acres. Apart from minor modifications around the entrances the perimeter of the Tower has not changed since the building of the Moat and outer walls by Edward I.

# VIII

# *The Royal Armouries*

In 1958 the Queen consented to the Armouries being given the title of 'Royal Armouries' in recognition of its long association with the monarchy and, of course, its status as one of the finest museums of arms and armour in the world. Arms and armour have always been held in the Tower but the Royal Armouries as we know them today derive from the reign of Henry VIII. Many of his soldiers' weapons and armour, as well as cannon which he commissioned, have been at the Tower ever since, and the King's own armours were later to be added.

Although immensely popular during earlier centuries, armour went out of fashion at the time of the first world war when the horrors of that conflict made any display of martial clothing almost scandalous. Additionally, the attractive display of Madame Tussaud-style dummies was abandoned in favour of transparent skeletal type display units, admirable for the experts but disastrous for viewing by the general public. Schoolchildren were bored and glamour was lost. The Royal Armouries has reversed this trend and now shows splendidly life-like figures which bring armour to life and recapture the history of the original owners. Armour should also be seen as an art and it is interesting that etching on steel plate, invented at the beginning of the sixteenth century, was originally for armour not print-making. The inlay work is superb, particularly with mother-of-pearl; even Holbein was commissioned by Henry VIII to design armour.

*Cannon on Tower Wharf.*

The modern visitor can be overwhelmed by the sheer quantity of the exhibits of the Royal Armouries, split as they are between the White Tower, the Oriental Armoury (Waterloo Block), the British Military Armoury (the New Armouries) and the Bowyer Tower. Those with children will be dragged off to see the torture instruments on display at the Bowyer Tower, together with the block and axe used for the last beheading on Tower Hill (Lord Lovat in 1747). For most visitors, it is essential to dine à la carte on the many treasures. Tastes differ but there is something for everyone; the museum caters for those whose knowledge is limited, or non-existent, but at the same time does not neglect the better informed.

The most famous exhibit of the Royal Armouries is undoubtedly the 1540 foot armour made for Henry VIII after his jousting accident. The codpiece was the subject of bawdy chat and, in the eighteenth century, ladies who wished to conceive would stick a pin into the codpiece—a practice that was stopped by the Archbishop of Canterbury. A poster showing this armour forms part of a modern advertising campaign on the London Underground system and still provokes ribald comments.

It is a great pity that visitors cannot see men wearing the armour and moving about, as the flexibility is remarkable; the joints move in a way that is difficult to describe—rather like a caterpillar. In the earlier days of space exploration scientists from the United States came to the Armouries to study the techniques used in sixteenth-century body armour as these were directly applicable to the making of space-suits. Most armour that we have was designed for tournaments and was often highly decorated to catch the eye of the ladies. There was a fashion in armour (e.g. square toes, pointed toes and rounded toes) and who would want to be seen wearing last year's scabbard? Many sword-blades are much older than their hilts and scabbards. Armour was also of two types, one for foot combat, the other for a mounted fight. An outstanding example of mounted armour is the set made for man and horse in the late fifteenth century, known as the Gothic armour. Displayed on model figures it has a tremendous impact on all visitors and is an impressive sight at the end of a gallery.

Not all sixteenth-century men were small, though on average they were shorter than today. One of the Keepers of the Royal Armouries is 6 feet 8 inches (just over 2 m) tall but finds the German armour, made in about 1535, too big for him. Armour was tailored for individuals, which makes it difficult to model as it is very uncomfortable if it does not fit. We found this when we persuaded a young girl secretary to dress up in a boy's armour for a television presentation. She was tiny and even in a boy's armour she had to wear high-heeled shoes. Another small suit of armour, some 38 inches (96 cm) high, was made in 1630, probably for Jeffrey Hudson the Queen's court dwarf, who was quite prepared to lead troops, despite his size. The 'frog-mouthed' jousting helm needs explanation. As the combatants galloped towards each other, they leant forward so that they could see through the gap in the helm; at the last moment, they straightened up so that the face was completely protected from a lance-blow. A small boy, not understanding this, said, 'Mummy, is that where they put the sandwiches in?'

The Royal Armouries has lately become well-known for its campaigns to retain historic pieces in the United Kingdom. It has achieved some remarkable successes in fund raising and the

*The 1540 foot armour made at Greenwich for Henry VIII.*

(Overleaf left) *Elephant in armour, probably captured by Clive of India at the Battle of Plassey in 1757.*

(Overleaf right) *Chris Smith of the Royal Armouries in Gothic style. South German, late 15th century.*

visitor should not miss the Earl of Southampton's armour (c. 1598) which is a marvellous example of rich etching. Southampton was the patron of William Shakespeare, and his armour would now be in an overseas collection were it not for the dedicated efforts of the Armouries staff to equal the foreign bid.

For a different sort of armour, the tourist should visit the Oriental Armoury where the first exhibit is also the largest—an elephant in armour. The first elephant in the Tower was presented to the Menagerie in 1255, but this armour dates probably from 1757, and was captured by Clive in India at the battle of Plassey. It is a great attraction for children of all ages. Also of particular interest is the 'before and after' demonstration, made possible by the Japanese government, who took one of two presentation armours given to James I in 1614 by the Governor of Edo (Tokyo) and had it completely restored to look as new. Side by side with the old, it makes a marvellous contrast and brings the collection alive.

Some of the Japanese swords are exceedingly sharp and took up to two years to make. The old methods have been forgotten and it is only recently that an American scientist managed to reproduce sword-blades of the same quality, by a slow hardening process which adds carbon at a much lower temperature than that normally used. The sword-blade consists of a soft iron core, giving strength and resilience, and a covering of steel, the edge of which is separately tempered before being ground to extreme sharpness. Moreover, both core and covering are made up of many layers of metal, produced by a complex process of forging.

Swords, muskets and pikes abound; of particular interest are some of the intricate designs used by craftsmen to decorate their pieces. Robert Hardy, the actor and also a Trustee of the Royal Armouries, has a favourite which I can commend; it is the small-sword made for the City of London to present to Vice Admiral Lord Collingwood, Nelson's second-in-command at the battle of Trafalgar (1805). In the event it was not presented as poor Collingwood died at sea on

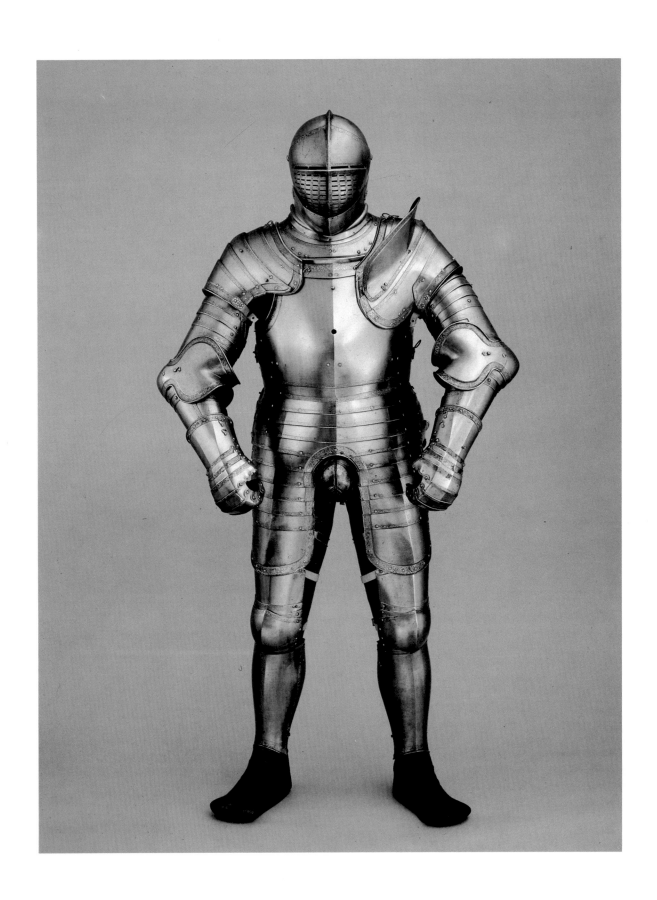

his way home to England.

The work of Grinling Gibbons and John Nost is represented by two wooden horses—one, a light dun (Gibbons), and the other, black (Nost). The dun (1685) was one of two made to carry the figures of Charles I and Charles II (the old Line of Kings), and the black was probably the mount of Henry VIII (made between 1688 and 1690). Another unusual sight, in the British Military Armoury, is the huge pediment that was rescued from the Grand Storehouse after the 1841 fire; after a multiplicity of small arms this enormous pediment comes as somewhat of a surprise.

The Royal Armouries is a very large modern museum and since the re-establishment of the post of 'Master of the Armouries' in 1935 it has achieved a character and momentum all of its

*The Armouries workshop.*

*This grotesque helmet is all that remains of the armour made for Henry VIII by the Court Armourer of Maximilian I, Konrad Seusenhofer.*

own. Latterly, in 1984, its control was transferred from the Department of the Environment to a new Board of Trustees, a major step forward as Civil Service financing is not suited to the cut and thrust of the auctioneers' world, where the Armouries can be both buyers and sellers at short notice. It is the only major museum that has been open to the public since 1661, and there is a certain irony in its headquarters, built in 1663–64, being called the *New* Armouries. In keeping with the name and to encourage modern weapon makers, the Royal Armouries commissioned a special shotgun engraved with a motif of ravens' feathers; the artist was the Scot, Malcolm Appleby. Traditional support for craftsmen continues and is an important function of the Royal Armouries, as it has been since Elizabethan times.

# IX
# *The Crown Jewels*

The display in the Waterloo Block of the Tower of London has always been known as the Crown Jewels. This can be misleading to visitors as it includes the Regalia used at a coronation, Church Plate, Banqueting Plate, and individual items that have been presented by past sovereigns or consorts. Their value is impossible to assess as no comparable items have come to auction; a guess estimate for the First Star of Africa, the largest diamond in the world, was some £80 million, but it could be worth more as large diamonds cannot be priced by conventional methods.

The essentials for the coronation ceremony do not change and date from the time of Edgar (943–75) who was crowned as the first King of all England in 973. All coronations have differences in detail as they reflect the wishes of the monarch at the time. Edward VII had a number of modifications made to help him through the ceremony, as he was far from well when he succeeded to the throne; other monarchs had variations to suit their taste in ways not dissimilar to any family wedding.

When a sovereign dies, the successor is proclaimed to the country ('The King is dead, long live the King!'), and preparations begin for the coronation, probably to take place some nine months later, although this period is variable. Since the reign of Queen Victoria the procession has taken a route from Buckingham Palace to Westminster Abbey, where the sovereign is met

*The Imperial State Crown, front.*

and escorted to the Chair of State. Selected individuals carry the processional objects (a special Court decides who carries what), beginning with two of the Royal Maces. These are ornate versions of old close-protection weapons, made of silver-gilt (solid silver gilded with gold), and carried by the sovereign's personal escort, the Sergeants-at-Arms. They are quite heavy, some 23 to 25 lb, and are a symbol of power. They are also used at the State Opening of Parliament, and three are permanently on loan, one each, to the House of Commons, the House of Lords and the Lord Chamberlain's Office.

Ahead of the new sovereign are carried three Swords of Justice, known as the Curtana (Sword of Mercy), Spiritual Justice, and Temporal Justice. These three swords are good examples of the practice of fitting an old blade with a new hilt and scabbard; though made for the coronation of Charles II in 1661, the blades are of a century earlier. Apart from a few items and historic jewels, the present Regalia dates from the Restoration of the monarchy in 1660. As explained in Chapter 4, Cromwell disposed of the previous Regalia by sale, or melting down for coinage.

After the three Swords of Justice follows the sovereign's official sword, the Great Sword of State; this is a seventeenth-century two-handed sword, first used for James II, and weighs about 8½ lb. This is also carried at the State Opening of Parliament, by a senior retired soldier, sailor, or airman, chosen by the sovereign—an awkward burden for anyone of advanced years, and a strap round the waist is used to help the sword arm.

St Edward's Staff, a long gold sceptre, is less of a burden; after the procession it is placed on the altar and has no further part in the ceremony. Its nearest symbolic equivalent is the pastoral staff of a bishop.

The sovereign is next presented to the people by way of an Acclamation. Then starts the Service of Holy Communion which is the basis of the ceremony. It is interrupted by the Anointing, the instruments being the Ampulla and the Spoon. The Ampulla is a golden eagle holding the anointing oil which is poured through the beak, into the Spoon. The Spoon is the oldest piece in the Regalia and dates from the coronation of King John (1199).

The sovereign is then dressed in the Coronation Robes, made of gold thread, and weighing some 23 lb. These were made for George IV in 1821 but Queen Elizabeth II found them very heavy—particularly when they fought against the pile of the carpet in Westminster Abbey. The Stole is modern: it was given to the Queen in 1953 by the nine Commonwealth nations of which she was then titular Head of State.

Then the Golden Spurs, representing chivalry, are placed on the altar after they have touched the heels of the sovereign. Although made in 1661 they follow a pre-thirteenth-century pattern for no better reason than that it was fashionable at the time. The personal sword, known as the Jewelled Sword, is then presented; it has a gold scabbard, some magnificent precious stones, and is said to be the most expensive sword in the world. The Treasury made George IV pay for it himself and in 1821 it cost £5,998. It would be worth many million pounds today.

New Armills (bracelets) were made for the 1953 coronation, again a present from the nine Commonwealth nations; they represent sincerity and wisdom. The Orb, representing the Christian sovereignty over the world, is placed in the sovereign's right hand and is thoroughly awkward to hold. Luckily it weighs only 2 lb 14 oz, but it is more suited to a man's hand than a

*The head of the Sceptre with the Cross, showing the largest diamond in the world – the First Star of Africa.*

woman's. When returned to the altar, it is replaced by the Sovereign's Ring (made for William IV in 1831) which is meant for the third finger of the right hand (i.e. the continental wedding finger). Queen Victoria's fingers were too tiny for her to use this ring and her mother, the Duchess of Kent, gave her an exact copy, which was meant to fit the wedding finger. Unfortunately the jeweller was told to make it for the fourth finger of the right hand (the old jewellers' count included the thumb) but he used the new count and made it for the little finger. The Archbishop forced it on to the wedding finger and Queen Victoria's diary reveals the pain and problems she had in removing it; it took two hours and a lot of ice.

Then follows the investing with the Sceptre with the Cross and the Sceptre with the Dove. The Cross represents the sovereign's temporal power, while the Dove symbolises equity and mercy. In the head of the Sceptre with the Cross is the First Star of Africa, the largest diamond in the world, of some 530 carats. (To put this in perspective, the Elizabeth Burton diamond weighs 69 carats, and the Hope Diamond 45.)

The crown used by the Archbishop of Canterbury to complete the ceremony is St Edward's Crown, weighing an ounce under 5 lb. It is of solid gold and set with semi-precious stones which date from the coronation of George V (before that, it was set with fresh stones for each coronation, these being hired from a jeweller at 4 per cent of the total value, and replaced later with crystals). It is conceivable that the lower half of this crown is that of Edward the Confessor, or the gold may have come from the old crown; certainly no cost was made for the gold other than for re-furbishing which was related to the arches.

The 'going-away hat' from Westminster Abbey is the Imperial State Crown, which is also worn for the State Opening of Parliament. This is outstanding, particularly under television lights, when the 2,800 diamonds give of their best; the fire of diamonds only shows when the viewer or the diamonds move. The State Crown is full of historic stones, all of which have been

The Prince of Wales Crown,
1728.

The Imperial State Crown from
the back, showing the Stuart
Sapphire (104 carats).

mentioned earlier in this book. In the Maltese Cross, at the top, is St Edward's Sapphire, taken from the finger of Edward the Confessor when his tomb was moved on 13 October 1163. Then there is the Black Prince's Ruby—a pierced semi-precious stone called a balas or spinel—the hole being filled by a true ruby: it was worn by Henry V at the battle of Agincourt (1415), and was nearly lost when the Duc d'Alençon made his famous charge, knocking the Crown from Henry's head. The Stuart Sapphire at the back of the Crown can be traced back to Alexander II of Scotland (1214); it used to be in the front until replaced in 1911 by the Second Star of Africa, the second largest diamond in the world of some 317 carats. The two big diamonds, the First and Second Stars of Africa, were cut from the Cullinan diamond (3,106 carats), found in the Premier Mine in South Africa in 1905; they are of the highest possible quality (i.e. flawless 'D'). Both huge diamonds can be clipped together to form a brooch, although the last time they were worn this way was by Queen Mary on 13 June 1914.

The Cullinan was cut into nine major diamonds and ninety-six minor (i.e. one, two, or three carats). The cutting was ordered by Edward VII, who was given the Cullinan in 1907, by the Transvaal Government, on his sixty-sixth birthday. Joseph Asscher, who did the first cleaving, was said to have fainted after the ordeal. His nephew, Louis Asscher, in a recent conversation with me, denied this and said that he had been asked by the Queen if the story were true; she visited the Asscher's workshops in Holland in 1958. His reply was 'Your Majesty, you would not expect the surgeon to faint after operating on your daughter' (Princess Anne had just had her appendix removed). In truth a bottle of champagne was opened which led to further celebrations. Edward VII retained Cullinans I and II (now the First and Second Stars of Africa) and gave the remainder to the cutters as payment, though he bought back Cullinan VI as a present for Queen Alexandra. In 1910 the other six big diamonds were bought by the Transvaal Government as a present for the Princess of Wales (later

*The crown made for the Prince of Wales (later George V) to wear at the coronation of Edward VII in 1902, and worn in turn by the Duke of Windsor as Prince of Wales at the coronation of George V in 1911.*

Queen Mary), who was to open the first Parliament of the Union of South Africa. The death of Edward VII in 1910 caused this engagement to be cancelled, but the diamonds were still presented to Queen Mary—at Marlborough House by the High Commissioner for the Union of South Africa. Cullinans III and IV were set in Queen Mary's Crown, but are now replaced by crystals, the two diamonds being made into a brooch often worn by Elizabeth II. They are the same shapes as Cullinans I and II, pear and cushion, but are only 94 and 64 carats respectively (these are the diamonds known in royal circles as 'Granny's chips'). Cullinan V (heart-shaped) is in a brooch, Cullinan VI is a drop pendant, Cullinans VII and VIII are set together in a brooch, and Cullinan IX is in a ring. Apart from Cullinans I and II, the seven remaining diamonds are the personal property of Elizabeth II. The Sovereign owns the State Collection, but only as Head of State; the jewellery worn by Elizabeth II is from her personal collection.

The Hanoverian pearls also belong to Elizabeth II and are worn by her and by the Queen Mother. Three of the four large pearls under the orb of the Imperial State Crown are likely to have been taken from them, the fourth being added by the Crown Jewellers—Rundell, Bridge & Rundell—in 1837. (This disproves the story that the four pearls in the Imperial State Crown were from earrings of Elizabeth I.) The history of the Hanoverian pearls is unusual. Pope Clement VII gave them to Catherine de Medici, on her marriage. She in turn gave them to Mary Queen of Scots when Mary married the Dauphin of France, Catherine's son. After Mary's execution Elizabeth I of England bought the pearls on valuation. They were described by the French Ambassador of the day, de la Fôret, as 'six long strings of pearls, with twenty-five single pearls as large as nutmegs'. The pearls passed from Elizabeth I to James I, who gave them to his daughter, Elizabeth of Bohemia. Her daughter was Sophia, the Electress of Hanover, and the pearls passed from her to her son, George I, and so on down to the present day.

Some other items of the collection which are

used, and are not just for display, include the very large Altar Dish (1664) which forms the centre-piece of the altar in Westminster Abbey at the time of the coronation. The main theme is the Last Supper but, unusually, there is a dog in the foreground. Perhaps this was because Charles II loved dogs—he introduced the King Charles Spaniel into this country. The Maundy Dish (1660) is used by the sovereign on Maundy Thursday (the Thursday before Easter) to distribute Maundy money to the needy in a ceremony relating to the biblical theme of humility. The ceremony takes place in a different cathedral each year. Maundy money is specially minted (silver 1d, 2d, 3d and 4d pieces), and, since the ceremony is related to the age of the monarch (in 1987 there were sixty-one purses for old men and sixty-one for old women), more dishes are frequently needed. Two dishes (c. 1661), each with a fish motif, are used for this. If the cathedral is by the sea the salt-water fish dish is used, if inland the fresh-water dish.

At Christmas, Easter and Whitsun, the 1691 Altar Dish and Flagon, presented to Lord Lucas, Constable of the Tower at that time, are placed on the altar in St Peter ad Vincula, as this is the time of the State Parades when the Resident Governor is escorted to the Chapel by the Yeoman Body, all in State Dress.

The other crowns on view are not normally used, although Queen Elizabeth the Queen Mother has had hers out for a portrait session. The Imperial State Crown of India (1911) has some 6,000 precious stones incorporated in its frame, and was used at the Delhi Durbar by George V when he was crowned King Emperor of India. Queen Mary's Crown was presented by her to the State, in 1914, as a future Consort's Crown. This posed a problem later since Queen Mary was present at the coronation of George VI in 1937 so a second crown had to be made for Queen Elizabeth (now the Queen Mother). Queen Mary broke with tradition to attend that coronation (hitherto the Queen Dowager had not gone to the coronation of her husband's successor). Her biographers imply that this was because she wanted to show family unity after

*The Education Department bringing history alive.*

the abdication of Edward VIII. She wore her own crown, less the arches, in the form of a circlet. Queen Elizabeth the Queen Mother followed the same pattern at the coronation of her daughter Elizabeth II in 1953, transforming her crown into a circlet, the arches being removable. The Koh-i-Noor Diamond was transferred from Queen Mary's Crown to Queen Elizabeth the Queen Mother's Crown; the frame of the latter is made of platinum, the only crown fashioned in this precious metal. It originally held the Lahore diamond in the Maltese cross above the orb, but this was relaced by a crystal, the diamond being used as a drop from a diamond collet necklace now worn by Elizabeth II. The stone below the Koh-i-Noor comes from a stomacher given to Queen Victoria by the Sultan of Turkey. After the 1937 coronation, Cullinans III and IV were taken from Queen Mary's Crown, where they were replaced by crystals, and were made into a brooch often worn by the Queen.

Perhaps the most unusual crown in the collection is the Small Crown of Queen Victoria (1870). It weighs only 4 oz and was made for her when she was fifty-one years old; it contains some 2,300 diamonds taken from an old fringe necklace. Queen Victoria was a tiny lady who hated the Imperial State Crown as she felt it was out of proportion to her height; also it was a nuisance to get it out of the Jewel House— crowns were worn much more then than they are today. Consequently, she wore the Small Crown frequently, and many pictures exist showing her with the crown perched on her bun hair style.

Mary of Modena's Crown and Diadem (1685) can best be understood by imagining a lady going to church. To get to Westminster Abbey for her coronation as James II's queen she needed a hat—the Diadem. The Coronation Crown remained in the Abbey (today the frame is in the Museum of London), but being now crowned she needed a better hat than the diadem to go home in—the 'Rich' Crown—so called because the original hired diamonds were valued at £110,000, an enormous sum for those days. It is now set with crystals.

The largest piece of Banqueting Plate is the

*Mr Melling, Curator of the
Crown Jewels.*

famous Wine Cooler (1829), often called the Grand Punch Bowl. It weighs nearly a quarter of a ton (8,000 oz) and is some 779 oz heavier than the silver Jerningham-Kandler wine cooler on display in the Hermitage in Leningrad. The decorative figures represent the wine harvest and, underneath, the sea caves; all these can be removed and number 134 separate pieces. In 1986 the Wine Cooler was completely stripped down for special cleaning but, despite all pre-cautions, on reassembly room could only be found for 133 pieces. It took two hours to find the empty hole. Queen Victoria decided to use the Wine Cooler as a punch bowl for the christening of her son, later to become Edward VII. For this the ladle (1841) was made and the Wine Cooler is often referred to as the Grand Punch Bowl.

In 1983, when the Queen of the Netherlands visited Queen Elizabeth II, the two Caddinets were sent to Windsor Castle because of their Dutch connection with William III and Mary II. They look rather like a pen and ink set but are, in fact, royal place settings. Salt was in the left-hand receptacle, implements in the right, vin-egar in the little jug, and a plate could be put on the stand. The insignia are interesting. The first Caddinet (1683) has William and Mary's usual coat of arms, with a Scottish Unicorn supporter, but the second (1689) has the Tudor Dragon. This is known as the 'No Scottish' period because the English Parliament offered the Crown to William and Mary on 13 February 1689, whereas the Scottish Parliament did not meet until 4 March, making their proclamation on 14 April. Tact demanded that Scotland should not be mentioned for these few weeks.

Salt was very important in the seventeenth century and it was also expensive. The Exeter Salt (1630), a castle with a lighthouse on top, was a present for Charles II, the city of Exeter having supported Cromwell, and now wanting to gain favour. Under each turret is a receptacle holding about an ounce of salt, and there are drawers and a drawbridge for spices. Johan Haas of Hamburg, who made the Salt, is said to have designed the castle to look like the White Tower

*The Exeter Salt.*

and added the Pharos of Alexandria (the light-house), the Seventh Wonder of the Old World, for good measure; this is a splendid explanation but probably too good to be true.

The St George's Salts have an interesting history. On 15 April 1661, the Knights of the Garter invited Charles II to a dinner in celebration of his return and to commemorate St George's Day—the date being as close to St George's Day (23 April) as the royal diary would permit. They ordered four Salts for the King's table (hour-glass shaped, with canopies), four sets of four cylinder-shaped Salts (a total of sixteen), again with canopies, for the Knights' tables or Messes, and a further four Salts for the Officers of the Order who were not Knights of the Garter (e.g. the Garter King of Arms). These Salts had no canopies, but were given napkin brackets so that a napkin could cover the salt. In 1681 twelve of the cylinder Salts were melted down, on the orders of Sir Gilbert Talbot—Charles II was running short of money again. A thirteenth disappeared at the coronation of William and Mary, the Elizabeth Salt (1572) being brought in to make up numbers. In 1821 George IV, determined to have the biggest and best coronation banquet ever, ordered the Crown Jewellers to put on a show. They turned out all the Banqueting Plate and when they came to the St George's Salts, they mistook the napkin brackets on the officers' set for legs, turned them upside-down, and said, 'My God, we've lost the innards!' They made new receptacles and these Salts were displayed upside-down for the next eighty years, until in 1906 William Watts of the Victoria and Albert Museum spotted the error.

The town of Plymouth had also supported Cromwell and wanted to put itself on the right side of Charles II by giving him a present, this time a fountain (1650) for use at table, probably to pour wine on sliced fruit. The wine came from the top figure and from the four figures around the stem. When the fountain was taken from the Jewel House for the coronation of George III it was signed for by Prince Frederick Ernst, Page of the Back Stairs at Buckingham Palace. When it was returned, it lacked the top figure, Hercules, which the Prince kept for a souvenir. A new top figure, Cleopatra and the Asp, had to be made for George IV's coronation banquet.

Fortnum & Mason, the famous London store in Piccadilly, has a link with the Crown collection. William Fortnum was a footman to Queen Anne and used to sell the candle ends from the two candlesticks (1662), now in the Jewel House, together with others from the Palace, to a grocer in Piccadilly called Hugh Mason—the first association of the two names. Later, Charles Fortnum, a footman at the Court of George III, on leaving royal service joined with the grandson of Hugh Mason to form the firm of Fortnum & Mason. When the clock outside the store strikes

the hour, a footman comes out on one side of it bearing a salver, and on the other side one bearing a candelabra.

A passing mention was made earlier of the Charles II Font (1660) but, it is not generally known, that the Alms Dish alongside it is not an alms dish at all, but the base of the font. Originally, the two were bolted together, but they proved heavy and too difficult to carry, so were separated. They make an interesting optical illusion as the base of the font fits exactly into the centre of the Alms Dish; it looks much too small to do this.

Finally, there are two Prince of Wales Crowns. The Hanoverian kings always hated their eldest sons. George II was in constant conflict with Prince Frederick Louis who refused to come to his father's coronation but then needed a crown in order to take his seat in the House of Lords. He therefore had one made in 1828 and it was put on a cushion in front of him whenever he attending a sitting. The crown was last used by Edward VII as nowadays the Prince of Wales does not take his seat in the House of Lords in that fashion. Frederick Louis died as the result of a blow from a tennis ball—an unusual end for an heir apparent. The other crown was made for George V as Prince of Wales for the coronation of Edward VII in 1902. It was next worn in 1911 by the future King Edward VIII (later the Duke of Windsor) at the coronation of his father George V. It then disappeared and was completely forgotten until it was found among the Duke's effects after his death.

There are many more items on display, but enough has been said to illustrate the size of the collection and to hint at its value. The Crown Jewels in the Tower are visited by everyone who wants to see something beyond price, steeped in history, and unique in this world. Like the Tower itself, they are part of our English heritage.

*The end of the day – Chief Yeoman Warder Harding on his way to close the Tower to the public.*

# Index

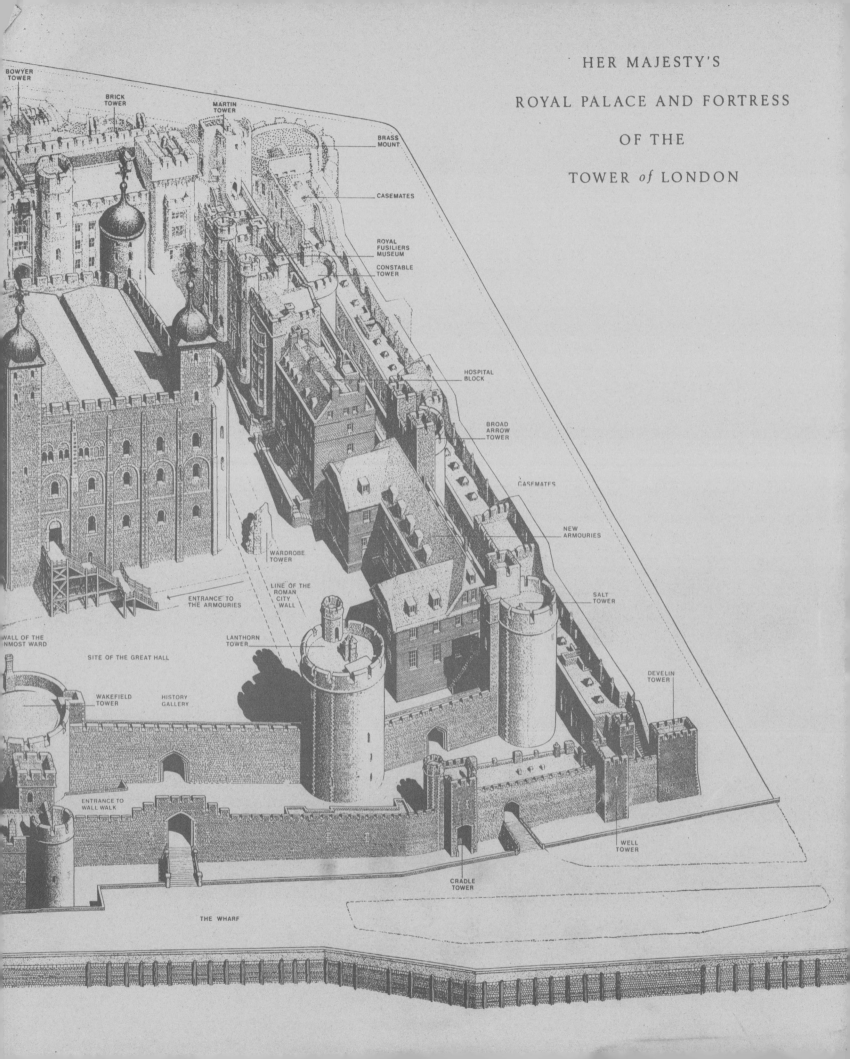

HER MAJESTY'S

ROYAL PALACE AND FORTRESS

OF THE

TOWER *of* LONDON

BOWYER TOWER

BRICK TOWER

MARTIN TOWER

BRASS MOUNT

CASEMATES

ROYAL FUSILIERS MUSEUM

CONSTABLE TOWER

HOSPITAL BLOCK

BROAD ARROW TOWER

CASEMATES

NEW ARMOURIES

SALT TOWER

WARDROBE TOWER

LINE OF THE ROMAN CITY WALL

ENTRANCE TO THE ARMOURIES

DEVELIN TOWER

WALL OF THE INMOST WARD

LANTHORN TOWER

SITE OF THE GREAT HALL

WAKEFIELD TOWER

HISTORY GALLERY

WELL TOWER

ENTRANCE TO WALL WALK

CRADLE TOWER

THE WHARF